Stirring the Nation's Heart

Eighteen Stories of
Prophetic Unitarians and Universalists
of the Nineteenth Century

Polly Peterson

Gail Forsyth-Vail
Developmental Editor

UNITARIAN UNIVERSALIST ASSOCIATION
BOSTON

Copyright © 2010 by the Unitarian Universalist Association of Congregations, 25 Beacon St., Boston, MA 02108. All rights reserved.

Printed in the United States

ISBN 1-55896-570-X
978-1-55896-570-6

14 13 12 11 10
5 4 3 2 1

Library of Congress Cataloging-in-Publication Data

Peterson, Polly, 1950-
Stirring the nation's heart : eighteen stories of prophetic Unitarians and Universalists of the nineteenth century / Polly Peterson ; Gail Forsyth-Vail, developmental editor.
   p. cm.
  ISBN-13: 978-1-55896-570-6 (pbk. : alk. paper)
  ISBN-10: 1-55896-570-X (pbk. : alk. paper)
  1. Unitarians—Biography. 2. Universalists—Biography. I. Forsyth-Vail, Gail. II. Title.
BX9867.P48 2010
289.1092'273—dc22
[B]
                        2010019719

"Going to Walden" is from *New and Selected Poems, Volume 1*, by Mary Oliver, copyright © 1992 by Mary Oliver, reprinted by permission of Beacon Press, Boston.

Contents

Introduction   v

NEW IDEAS ABOUT RELIGION

Julia Ward Howe's Liberal Faith	1
Unitarian Apostle William Ellery Channing	10
Ralph Waldo Emerson and the Birth of Transcendentalism	19
Henry David Thoreau's Search for Higher Truth	29
Judith Sargent Murray and American Universalism	40

NEW IDEAS ABOUT EDUCATION

Bronson Alcott and Elizabeth Palmer Peabody's Educational Reform	53
Margaret Fuller's New View of Womanhood	65
Making the Ideal Real at Brook Farm	77

ABOLITION OF SLAVERY

Lydia Maria Child Battles Racism with Her Pen	89
Antislavery Poet and Orator Frances Ellen Watkins Harper	101
Theodore Parker and the Fugitive Slave Law	113
Robert Gould Shaw and the Fifty-fourth Massachusetts Regiment	124

WOMEN'S RIGHTS

Lucy Stone and Henry Blackwell Redefine Marriage	133
Susan B. Anthony's Challenges and Devotion	144
Olympia Brown Gets the Vote	156

CONCERN FOR THE DISPOSSESSED

Minister-at-Large Joseph Tuckerman 167
Samuel Gridley Howe's Equal Opportunity for All Children 177
Dorothea Dix Fights for People with Mental Illness 187

Introduction

Unitarian Universalism does not rest on the religious authority of a particular creed, a sacred text, or a specific dogma, but rather on ideas of freedom—freedom of thought and freedom of conscience—and on the notion that we are all connected one to another and to the larger world. Unitarian Universalists are people who question and wonder—congregations of lifelong learners who draw lessons and inspiration from a wide variety of secular and religious sources. We commit to exploring our faith in a community of fellow seekers with whom we share certain fundamental principles and understandings, but we also understand that we will probably not all follow exactly the same paths or reach the same conclusions. We believe that our faith calls us to work for justice, but we know that the work will take many forms.

Critics may say this approach is too broad, too vague, or too rootless to have any real meaning. The criticism would not be new. "Belief? they have no belief," railed an outraged conservative against the Massachusetts Unitarians when William Ellery Channing was allowed to speak in New York in 1820. "They are a paradox; you cannot fathom them. How can you fathom a thing that has no bottom?"

Yet people who cherish the right to think for themselves and who wish to confront the world's challenges with hearts wide open find a broad-minded, far-reaching approach to religious ideas richly rewarding. This book explores the nineteenth-century roots of our liberal faith through the stories of some of the people who led us in new directions at a pivotal time in American history.

The Puritan Past

In the eighteenth century, American colonists rebelled against the authority of British rule and established a new nation, whose founding principles of liberty, individual rights, and freedom from tyranny had profound implications for religion. Meanwhile, a quiet rebellion was also taking place against the Calvinist orthodoxy of the Congregational churches of New England. Liberal ministers in Massachusetts were rejecting the old creeds. A small congregation of dissenters in Gloucester was fighting a legal battle for separation of church and state. These rebellious New Englanders were our Unitarian and Universalist forebears.

The Calvinist beliefs and structures they were rebelling against were brought to America in the 1620s by the founders of the first English settlements in Massachusetts. The original colonists were radical Protestants from the Church of England who wanted to remove all traces of Roman Catholicism from their Christian worship. Most of them were Puritans, whose beliefs were based on the ideas of John Calvin, a sixteenth-century French theologian.

The important tenets of Calvinism seem foreign to Unitarian Universalists today. They included these ideas:

- God is all-powerful and reveals himself in three parts: Father, Son, and Holy Spirit.
- Because of the original sin of Adam, as told in the Bible, all infants are born sinners.
- By his death, Jesus Christ redeemed the souls of some sinners, but salvation is not for everyone. God has already chosen the "elect"—the people who will be saved; all others will suffer eternal damnation. God's choice is unchangeable and forever.
- Faith is more important than good works. Salvation does not depend on the actions of the sinner but is by God's grace alone.

As the number of colonial settlements in Massachusetts grew, each town was required to establish a church that followed Calvinist doctrines. Although everyone was expected to attend church, not every colonist was a church member. Church membership and political leadership were reserved for those who had experienced a conversion—evidence of the workings of God's grace in their souls. These people were deemed to be among God's elect.

Under the Congregational system in Massachusetts, each church was independent. Each congregation drew up a covenant that served as the foundation for the religious life of the community, but since covenants rarely included specific points of dogma, there was considerable latitude for beliefs to change over time without any need to rewrite the covenant. In addition, each church had authority to choose its own minister. Because there was no higher denominational or ecclesiastical power, it was possible for an individual church to choose a minister with new ideas, whether or not neighboring churches agreed with those ideas.

The Rise of Unitarianism

In the eighteenth century, the requirements for church membership relaxed somewhat in many communities, and political privileges were no longer restricted to members. Meanwhile, a variety of Christian sects arose in Massachusetts alongside the official Standing Order of Congregational Churches. Still, there was no official separation of church and state, and all citizens, even those who belonged to independent churches outside the Standing Order, were required to support the Congregational Church and its ministers through taxes. In 1782, members of Gloucester's Independent Church of Christ, the first Universalist church in America, sued for the right to have their tax money go to their own church rather than to the local Congregational church. They won this right for themselves and for other nonconforming churches in Massachusetts in 1786, but Massachusetts did not officially sever the union of church and state until 1833. It was the last state in the union to do so.

This distinctive history helps explain the powerful presence of Unitarian churches in Massachusetts in the early nineteenth century. Unlike Universalism, which was a new sect trying to gain a foothold alongside the established Congregational churches, Unitarianism grew up from within those established churches. By the beginning of the nineteenth century, many Congregational churches in Massachusetts had chosen ministers who represented a way of thinking about religion that differed from Calvinism in some important respects. Their ideas were influenced by Enlightenment ideals, which emphasized rational thought, and European Romanticism, which viewed God as a loving father. Ministers who embraced the new outlook became known as liberal ministers, while those who maintained strictly Calvinist beliefs were known as orthodox.

For a while, official collegial relationships, such as pulpit exchanges, continued between ministers with orthodox and liberal positions, but when the most prestigious religious professorship at Harvard College went to a liberal minister in 1805, a heated pamphlet war began. The second story in this book, about William Ellery Channing, describes this great controversy and the important moment in 1819 when many of the liberal ministers within the Congregational establishment accepted that they had become a distinct group called Unitarians.

Soon, the churches in many Massachusetts parishes were Unitarian, including twenty of the twenty-five oldest churches in the commonwealth. In communities that had chosen Unitarian ministers, the dissenting orthodox church members sometimes broke away to establish separate congregations. As keepers of the old traditions, they hoped to maintain their status as the official church, but the Massachusetts Supreme Court ruled in 1820 that church property belonged to the group that represented the majority of voters in the parish, whether orthodox or Unitarian.

Although they had established a very powerful presence in Massachusetts, many Unitarians, including Channing, disliked sectarianism and were opposed to the founding of a new denomination. Unitarian ministers established the American Unitarian Association in 1825, but because of a general ambivalence around the issue of sectarianism, efforts by the national organization to expand Unitarianism outside Massachusetts were minimal.

The Rise of Universalism

In the early years of American Universalism, ministers traveled from town to town to preach. The first Universalist minister to settle in a church was John Murray, who became minister to America's first Universalist congregation in Gloucester, Massachusetts, in 1779. He was called to a congregation in Boston in 1793. The Universalists, like the Baptists and the Methodists, attracted followers in many towns and cities and were especially strong in rural areas. Because of their very different history, Universalists were less likely to be at the center of political power and cultural influence than Unitarians.

Hosea Ballou, who lived from 1771 to 1852, was the most influential Universalist minister of the generation that followed Murray. Although he preached in Boston at the same time as William Ellery Channing, the two appear to have had no relationship, apart from occasional written disagreements about doctrine. Like Channing, Ballou rejected the doctrine of the Trinity and placed great stress on the use of reason. He and Channing agreed on many other points as well, especially that of God's loving nature, but there is no evidence that they ever met face-to-face. Perhaps this was because Ballou was a rough-hewn, self-educated preacher, very unlike the Harvard men who filled Unitarian pulpits, and Channing did not wish to be associated with him. Perhaps it was because his style and tone too closely resembled the highly emotional appeals of the evangelical revivals that Unitarians condemned. Perhaps it was because his core beliefs were founded on the idea of man's inherent sinfulness, an idea that Unitarians firmly rejected. Whatever the reason, Universalism and Unitarianism in New England seem to have traveled along separate paths in the early nineteenth century, rarely encountering one another. Thomas Starr King (1824–1864), a gifted young minister who preached in both Universalist and

Unitarian churches, was the rare exception. It was not until people of both faiths were swept up in the reform movements of the 1850s and beyond—most notably in the campaign for women's rights—that Unitarians and Universalists worked closely together.

The Emergence of Transcendentalism

No sooner had the Unitarians established their own association than they too faced challenges from within. Young Unitarian ministers—Ralph Waldo Emerson, George Ripley, Theodore Parker, and others—expressed beliefs about human nature and the authority of the Bible that were more radical than the Unitarian beliefs of Channing's generation. This group, which became known as the Transcendentalists, challenged the emphasis on reason within Unitarianism and sought a spirituality that included the importance of intuition as a way to understand God. They looked to Channing as their guiding light, but they disagreed with him on some points. In their search for truth, they turned to sources such as ancient Greek philosophy and Asian religions, as well as the Bible. They believed that the divine spirit was present in every person and in all of nature, and that a direct relationship of each individual with God empowered human beings to improve themselves. This belief led many Transcendentalists to work not only for self-improvement but also for social change in harmony with a good and just God.

A Climate for Reform

The exciting ideas emerging during the 1830s and 1840s, especially among the Transcendentalists and their friends, came to be known as the "new views," "new thought," or simply "the newness." In the decades preceding the Civil War, Christian liberals began to emphasize deeds, not doctrines. The titles of William Ellery Channing's sermons catalog many of the concerns that reform-minded Unitarians addressed: "Self-Culture," "On the Elevation of the

Laboring Classes," "Ministry for the Poor," "Address on Temperance," "Remarks on Associations," "Lecture on War," and "Remarks on the Slavery Question."

In his 1859 reminiscence, Theodore Parker described the years from 1834 to 1840—the years of his theological study—as "the most interesting period of New England's spiritual history." He wrote,

> Dr. Channing was in the full maturity of his powers; and, after long preaching the dignity of human nature as an abstraction . . . , began to apply his sublime doctrines to actual life—in the individual, the State, and the Church. In the name of Christianity the Great American Unitarian called for the reform of the drunkard, the elevation of the poor, the instruction of the ignorant, and, above all, for the liberation of the American slave. Horace Mann, with his coadjutors, began a great movement to improve the public education of the people. The brilliant genius of Emerson rose in the winter nights, and hung over Boston, drawing the eyes of ingenuous young people to look up to that great new star—a beauty and a mystery. The rights of labor were discussed with deep philanthropic feeling and sometimes with profound thought. Mr. George Ripley, . . . one of the best cultured and most enlightened men in America, made an attempt at Brook Farm so to organize society that the results of labor should remain in the workman's hand. The natural rights of women began to be inquired into, and publicly discussed. I count it a piece of good fortune that I was a young man when these things were taking place; when great questions were discussed, and the public had not yet taken sides.

Unitarians and Universalists were leaders in the major social reforms of the nineteenth century. The stories in this book attempt to capture the spirit of that age and the new ideas that laid the groundwork for beliefs we hold today about religion, education, and social justice.

Organization of the Book

The core of this book is a set of eighteen read-aloud stories that tell about the ideas and achievements of famous Unitarians and Universalists. Each story begins with an introduction that helps set the story in its historical context, often linking it to other stories in the book. These introductions provide helpful background to anyone who plans to read or tell the stories aloud. Following each story is a selection of quotations by and about the subject of the story. They will expand readers' familiarity with our nineteenth-century forebears and give a clear sense of how the people of the time actually expressed themselves. The quotations provide a more in-depth basis for discussion than the story alone. Suggestions for using the story in a faith community and at home follow the quotations. The quotations and activity suggestions provide a starting point for applying knowledge about the past to a better understanding of the present. They also suggest ways to use the stories for self-reflection and growth.

The stories are organized around the following five themes:

New Ideas about Religion

The stories in the first section tell about the birth of liberal religion in America, with special emphasis on Transcendentalism. Although most of the Transcendentalists, and certainly Channing himself, identified as Christians, the Transcendentalists looked both to nature and to the great non-Western faith traditions as possible paths to religious understanding. At the heart of Transcendentalism was a desire to find moral and spiritual universals. Also at its heart was a belief that divinity exists within each person—an idea that helped to foster new ideas about equality. The last story in the section, which takes us back in time to the story of Judith Sargent Murray and the beginnings of Universalism in America, shows how the doctrine of universal salvation led Universalists to similar conclusions about human equality.

New Ideas about Education
Transcendental beliefs about human nature had profound implications for education. The first story in this section describes the progressive educational ideas of Bronson Alcott and Elizabeth Peabody, whose practices were grounded in Transcendentalist ideals. The second story explains how Margaret Fuller applied some of Alcott's educational ideas, along with her own remarkable conversational and intellectual skills, to create a new forum for the advancement of women. The last story in the section discusses Brook Farm, one of the most remarkable of the many experiments in communitarian living that emerged during this time of social and intellectual ferment. At Brook Farm, some of the great minds of the age applied their ideals to lifelong learning, as well as to an innovative approach to educating the young.

Abolition of Slavery
This section features Lydia Maria Child, Frances Ellen Watkins Harper, Theodore Parker, and Robert Gould Shaw—Unitarians who committed themselves in various ways to the abolition of slavery in the United States. Although individual Unitarians contributed greatly to the cause of abolition, it was an extremely divisive issue for Unitarian congregations. Slavery had long been illegal in New England, but the fortunes of many Unitarian merchants and industrialists still depended directly or indirectly upon slave labor. As a result, many Unitarian ministers were reluctant to take a stand on this issue for fear of losing the support of their parishioners. Eventually, William Ellery Channing did take an antislavery stand, and many of the other Unitarians featured in this book—Ralph Waldo Emerson, Henry David Thoreau, Julia Ward Howe, Samuel Gridley Howe, Bronson Alcott, Lucy Stone, and Susan B. Anthony—took active roles in the antislavery movement, along with those who are featured in the antislavery stories. Some of them were committed to nonviolence, while others believed slavery would be ended only by force. Four Massachusetts Unitarians—Thomas Wentworth Higginson, Theodore Parker,

Frank Sanborn, and Samuel Gridley Howe—were members of the Secret Six, a group that helped to fund John Brown's raid on the arsenal at Harper's Ferry, an action considered by many to be the opening salvo of the American Civil War.

Women's Rights

New ideas about human nature and education had a profound impact on attitudes toward equality of the sexes, but it was the antislavery movement that gave birth to the women's rights movement in a more direct and practical way. Women were prominent among early antislavery activists, and many of them became keenly aware of women's disenfranchisement as they advocated rights for enslaved African Americans. They also experienced overt discrimination themselves. They were denied delegate status at antislavery conventions. They were criticized, harassed, and threatened with violence for having the audacity to write and speak publicly. They had no power to change discriminatory laws. Meanwhile, antislavery societies were providing a number of women the opportunity to make a career of public speaking. It was not long before some of them began speaking publicly on the issue of women's rights. The three women featured in this section—Lucy Stone, Susan B. Anthony, and Olympia Brown—gave the fight for women's rights first priority in their careers. Brown was also the first woman to be ordained as a Universalist minister and one of the first female ministers in America, reminding us that Universalists were true pioneers in opening the ministry to women.

Concern for the Dispossessed

By the early nineteenth century, Unitarians and Universalists had rejected the notion that people's troubles are the will of God. Believing in the inherent worth of every person, something that Channing had called "likeness to God," they turned their energies toward seeking solutions to human misery. Joseph Tuckerman's story describes one of the very first acts of the American Unitarian Association in the 1820s: the establishment of a ministry-at-large to serve the poor of Boston. The next story features Samuel Gridley Howe, a Unitarian with an almost unbounded enthusiasm for aiding those whose lives placed them at a disadvantage, and outlines his remarkable achievements as the director of the first school for blind children in America. The last story discusses Dorothea Dix, a dedicated advocate for people with mental illness.

Unitarian Universalists have a long history of deep engagement with the challenges of their times. This book traces that dedication to its roots in the exciting decades of the nineteenth century known as "the newness." Lydia Maria Child reminisces about those days in a letter she wrote to an old friend and fellow abolitionist:

> The Holy Spirit *did* actually descend upon men and women in tongues of flame. Political and theological prejudices, and personal ambitions, were forgotten in sympathy for the wrongs of the helpless, and in the enthusiasm to keep the fire of freedom from being extinguished on our national altar. *All* suppression of selfishness makes the moment great: and mortals were never so sublimely forgetful of self, than were the abolitionists in those early days. . . . Ah, my friend, that is the *only* true church organization, when heads and hearts unite in working for the welfare of the human-race.

People often imagine that "once upon a time" society's problems were easier to understand and easier to solve. Yet one has only to reflect upon nineteenth-century American life to know that, whatever our troubles, Americans faced equally daunting challenges in the past. No incivility today can exceed the rancor of public discourse concerning slavery or woman suffrage. Economic collapses were just as devastating then as now. Poverty and ignorance were surely as widespread then and as seemingly intractable. The impact of immigration in those days was immense. The need to reform educational practices and to provide opportunities for disadvantaged people was by no means less pressing, and solutions were no easier to find. We can draw inspiration from the ways in which the

Unitarians and Universalists featured in this book faced the difficulties of their personal lives and the challenges of their time. May they help us live lives of personal reflection and social action with similar integrity, optimism, and courage in our own time.

New Ideas about Religion

Julia Ward Howe's Liberal Faith

Julia Ward Howe (1819–1910) had an extraordinary education for a girl of her day. Though she received little encouragement for her scholarly aspirations, she had a self-driven passion for learning and a wealthy father who was able to provide her with tutors, books, and a little private schooling. By the time she reached her teens, she was a serious student of languages, literature, philosophy, and music, and while in her teens, she published two scholarly papers. Then, at the age of twenty, a time of grief overwhelmed her. She turned to religion—to a strict form of Calvinist Christianity—but it gave her no comfort. A girlhood friend offered Howe some advice that expanded her religious outlook and helped change the trajectory of her life. As Howe later put it, "I studied my way out of all the mental agonies which Calvinism can engender and became a Unitarian."

Julia Ward Howe's story seems a fitting way to begin because the evolution of her thoughts and the events of her life encompass at a personal level many of the important changes taking place in nineteenth-century America as people began to think about God, human nature, and society in fundamentally new ways.

Julia Ward Howe was an enormously famous person in her time. She was so famous that when she died, thousands of people packed Boston's Symphony Hall for her memorial service, and hundreds more had to be turned away. They sang "The Battle Hymn of the Republic," a much-loved patriotic song that had first put Julia Ward Howe on the road to fame, and they celebrated her long and remark-

1

able life. But this story is not about the famous things she did. It's not about her poetry or her public speaking. It's not about her work to end slavery, her pleas for world peace, her tireless campaign for women's rights, or her preaching from Unitarian pulpits. It's about how she came to be the kind of person who would do those things.

Julia Ward was an unusual child right from the start. She was a high-spirited, precocious little red-haired girl, born in 1819 to wealthy parents. In those days, New York City was nothing like today's crowded metropolis filled with skyscrapers. Families like the Wards lived in big houses with private yards.

Julia had two older brothers, but she spent most of her time with her mother, who loved books and often read to her. Julia learned how to read both English and French at an early age. She and her mother enjoyed music and taking trips in their fancy horse-drawn carriage. But Julia's happy days with her mother soon came to an end. When she was five years old, her mother died.

Julia's father turned to strict Calvinist Christianity after his wife's death. By that time the family had grown; Julia had a third brother and two little sisters. To ensure that none of his children fell into evil ways, Mr. Ward made all sorts of rules. They were not allowed to go to the theater. They were not allowed to go to friends' houses. They were not allowed to play cards. Mr. Ward hired private tutors for his daughters so that they wouldn't have to go to school outside the home. On Sundays, they attended two long church services as well as Sunday school, and for the rest of the day, their reading was restricted to religious books. Though Julia loved her father, he often felt to her like a jailer.

When Julia was thirteen, she and her sisters and brothers began spending summers at the shore in Rhode Island, where life was more relaxed, and they could make new friends. There she found a best friend, a girl from Boston named Mary Ward. The two shared a passion for literature and learning.

Julia began making trips to Boston to visit Mary. In one of her letters to Mary, she referred to Boston as "an oasis in the desert, a place where the larger proportion of people are living, rational, and happy. I long for its green pastures and still waters, its pure intellectual atmosphere and its sunlight of kindness and truth."

When Mary became engaged to Julia's brother Henry, it appeared that these two best friends were destined to become sisters as well. Then suddenly, Julia's father died, and his death was followed only months later by that of her dear Henry.

Julia was devastated by the anguish of her double loss. She plunged into a terrible state of grief. Her oldest brother, Sam, had married and left home, and now that Henry was gone, Julia had become head of the household. She hadn't taken her father's religion very seriously before; but now, at the age of twenty, she embraced it with extreme zeal, ignited in part by a great religious revival going on in New York City. She joined a Bible study group and began distributing religious pamphlets. Calvinist teachings of hellfire and eternal damnation filled her mind with fear and guilt. She insisted on religious observances in the home that were even stricter than those her father had enforced, and she wrote poems filled with darkness and gloom.

In Boston, Mary's life was very different. She too had suffered a severe loss in Henry's death, but she had maintained her equilibrium. Her brother Sam belonged to a circle of friends known as the Transcendentalists, and she herself was among a group of women who attended Conversations led by Margaret Fuller. She heard lectures by Ralph Waldo Emerson and other optimistic and idealistic thinkers. Appalled by the desperate turn in Julia's outlook on life, Mary wrote her a letter in 1841, urging her to return to a more balanced way of thinking.

Along with the letter, Mary sent a sermon by the famous Unitarian minister William Ellery Channing. The subject of the sermon was the "church universal." Truth is not to be found in any one sect or creed, Channing declared. It is found in the common hopes and aspirations of all people who live with a pure and generous spirit, in all times and all places.

"I want you to step out of the religious atmosphere in which so much of your life has been passed," Mary wrote, "and for a moment, at least, to look abroad upon the church Universal towards which the spirit of the age and of the best and most enlightened men of the age is so strongly tending. That you will still adhere to all that is Holy and True in your particular church I believe but for God's sake let us seek to separate the chaff from the wheat—purge away the old heaven of bigotry and intolerance and God grant that the truth may indeed make us free."

As Mary had hoped, Julia soon freed herself from the grip of religious orthodoxy. While rereading John Milton's poem *Paradise Lost*, she suddenly realized that she no longer believed in the power of Satan. She felt certain that eternal evil was impossible and later wrote, "I threw away, once and forever, the thought of the terrible hell which had always formed part of my belief." For Julia, a loving God had replaced the "angry and vengeful Deity" of Calvinism.

Julia began to enjoy a lively social life in fashionable New York society, and she began making visits to Boston again. New Yorkers generally detested the ideas of Boston liberals—of abolitionists and Transcendentalists, of Channing and the Unitarians. But Julia found herself drawn to them more and more. On visits to Mary, she met Ralph Waldo Emerson and Margaret Fuller. She heard Channing preach. The tide turned for certain when she visited the Perkins Institution for the Blind and met its dashing director, Samuel Gridley Howe, the man she married in 1843. By marrying this well-known activist and reformer, she married herself to the reform movements of Boston. Through him, she met the Transcendentalist ministers Theodore Parker and James Freeman Clarke, who became her mentors in religious thought. Through him, she became involved in the antislavery movement. And no doubt because of him too, she joined the battle for women's rights. Despite his progressive social ideals, Samuel Gridley Howe's views on the proper role of a wife were oppressive and stifling, and the women's movement gave her a new sense of herself "as a free agent, fully sharing with man every human right and every human responsibility."

Julia Ward Howe occupied a special position in American society. As an intellectual, a free thinker, a published author, and a public speaker, she defied social conventions. None of these activities were considered proper for a married woman, yet she never lost her respectability. Confident in her own beliefs, Julia Ward Howe made reform respectable and helped change forever women's role in society. At the center of it all was her abiding religious faith—a faith she experienced not as dogma or a restrictive set of rules but as a guiding light. Her achievements were a testament to the power of free religious thought.

Quotations for Discussion

After Julia Ward Howe's death in 1910, her daughter Maud wrote a remembrance of her called *The Eleventh Hour in the Life of Julia Ward Howe*. After describing the many ways in which her mother kept her intellect keen throughout her long life, she asserts that her mother's intellect was only the secondary source of her power:

> What was it fed the inner flame of her life so that it shone through her face, as fire shines through an alabaster vase? She tapped the great life current that flows round the world; to those who know the trick, 'tis the simplest, most natural thing in the world to do. . . . You have merely to put yourself "on the circuit," let the force universal flow through you, and you can move mountains or bridge oceans. . . . Her first waking act was prayer, aspiration; her last, thanksgiving, praise! Just as some persons' first action is to open the window and fill the lungs with fresh air, or to drink a glass of cold water, hers was to open wide the door of her soul and let the breath of the Spirit blow through it.

Discussion: The words of Julia Ward Howe's daughter help us understand how deeply spiritual she was in her approach to life, even as she worked tirelessly for social justice. How is spirituality connected to social justice work in your own life?

In 1870, Julia Ward Howe worked to establish an International Women's Day for Peace. Horrified by the senseless slaughter of the Franco-Prussian War in Europe, she wrote her "Appeal to Womanhood throughout the World," which reads in part,

> Again have the sacred questions of international justice been committed to the fatal mediation of military weapons. In this day of progress, in this century of light, the ambition of rulers has been allowed to barter the dear interests of domestic life for the bloody exchanges of the battle-field. Thus men have done. Thus men will do. But women need no longer be made a party to proceedings which fill the globe with grief and horror. . . . Arise, then, Christian women of this day! Arise, all women who have hearts, whether your baptism be that of water or of tears! Say firmly: "We will not have great questions decided by irrelevant agencies. Our husbands shall not come to us, reeking with carnage, for caresses and applause. Our sons shall not be taken from us to unlearn all that we have been able to teach them of charity, mercy and patience. We, women of one country, will be too tender of those of another country, to allow our sons to be trained to injure theirs."

A few years later, after being disappointed in her hopes of establishing a world peace congress, Howe decided to establish a festival called Mother's Day that would be devoted to the advocacy of peace. She and her friends made it an annual observance on the second day of June. She never fully dedicated herself to the cause of peace, though. She had lived through a bloody civil war that brought an end to slavery in the United States, and to the end of her life, she supported wars that she considered just. At a peace conference in 1904, after hearing a talk that described the Buddhist beliefs and peaceful meditative practices of the Tibetan people, she said, "Mr. President and dear friends, assembled in the blessed cause of Peace, let me remind you that there is one word even more holy than peace, namely, justice.... The impulse which causes men to contend against injustice is a divine one, deeply implanted in the human breast. It would be wrong to attempt to thwart it."

Discussion: Some of the issues which concerned Howe are still alive for us today. Do you believe, as she did, that women bring a different perspective than men to questions of war and peace? How do you respond to her statement that justice is more holy than peace? Do you agree? Is war ever justified?

☙

In a speech called "What Is Religion?" that she delivered as part of the Parliament of World Religions at the Chicago World's Fair in 1893, Julia Ward Howe said,

> I think nothing is religion which puts one individual absolutely above others, and surely nothing is religion which puts one sex above another. Religion is primarily our relation to the Supreme, to God himself. It is for him to judge; it is for him to say where we belong, who is highest and who is not; of that we know nothing. And any religion which will sacrifice a certain set of human beings for the enjoyment or aggrandizement or advantage of another is no religion. It is a thing which may be allowed, but it is against true religion. Any religion which sacrifices women to the brutality of men is no religion.

Discussion: As a society, we still struggle with the inequalities that Howe identifies. How does contemporary Unitarian Universalist religious understanding support the ongoing struggle for justice? Do you agree with her understanding that God alone decides where we belong, or would you make a different religious argument in support of justice and equality?

Connecting with Our Lives

In Our Faith Communities

People often have complicated personal religious histories. Find members of your congregation—or other people of faith you know—who are willing to be interviewed about their religious past and how they came to be where they are on their faith journeys. You might want to record these interviews, either in writing or by audio or video recorder, and share them with your community.

Mary Ward asked Julia to step outside her long-held beliefs to consider a different religious outlook. Invite a small group or a youth group to discuss when it is good or necessary to consider alternatives to long-held practices or points of view and when it is appropriate for friends to help us do that. Ask them to discuss times they have done something beyond what is comfortable that has helped them grow and whether they have ever helped someone else do the same. Encourage one another to stretch a comfort zone by doing something unfamiliar or exploring something from a new perspective.

At Home

This story shows how people and ideas helped shape Julia Ward Howe's life. Try writing a journal entry, short memoir, or other piece about the influences in your life and how they have affected you. Alternatively, you can use another creative medium such as drawing or music.

Talk about how friends can help friends. What are some ways you have been supported when you were down and ways in which you have supported others? Would you ever send a sermon or a book that you thought might help a friend who is sad, depressed, or very ill? Has anyone ever done something similar for you?

Find Out More

Clifford, Deborah Pickman. *Mine Eyes Have Seen the Glory: A Biography of Julia Ward Howe*. Boston: Little, Brown, 1979.

Goodwin, Joan. "Julia Ward Howe." *Dictionary of Unitarian and Universalist Biography*, published online by the Unitarian Universalist Historical Society at www25.uua.org/uuhs.

Howe, Julia Ward. *Reminiscences, 1819–1899*. Boston: Houghton Mifflin, 1899. It can be read online at Google Books.

Howe, Maud. *The Eleventh Hour in the Life of Julia Ward Howe*. Boston: Little, Brown, 1911. It can be read online at Google Books.

Richards, Laura E., and Maud Howe Elliott. *Julia Ward Howe: 1819–1910, Vols. I and II*. Boston: Houghton Mifflin, 1915. It is available in the digital library of University of Pennsylvania.

Williams, Gary. *Hungry Heart: The Literary Emergence of Julia Ward Howe*. Amherst: University of Massachusetts Press, 1999.

Ziegler, Valarie H. *Diva Julia: The Public Romance and Private Agony of Julia Ward Howe*. Harrisburg, PA: Trinity Press International, 2003.

Unitarian Apostle
William Ellery Channing

William Ellery Channing (1780–1842) is known as the spiritual father of Unitarianism in America. He is the rock on which we stand, although physically, he was more like a slender reed, small in stature, with chronically ill health. His power lay in his character, his generosity, his clarity of thought, and his way with words. He became the minister of the Federal Street Church in Boston in 1803 and remained in that pulpit throughout his career. As a minister, he had a quiet authority and an almost saintly presence. As a writer, he gained the respect of the literary world, both in Europe and the United States. At his death, Theodore Parker said of him, "No man in America has left a sphere of such wide influence, no man since Washington has done so much to elevate his country."

This story focuses on the important moment in history when Channing's words gave birth to American Unitarianism as a distinct religious body, but many other stories in the book bear his stamp. He provided a foundation in religious thought for the emergence of Transcendentalism, for new ideas in education, for arguments against slavery, and for reforms aimed at improving the lives of the dispossessed. He was a generation older than most of the men and women featured in this book. Many of them looked to him as the spiritual guide of their formative years.

There was a war going on in New England in the early 1800s—a war fought not with guns or swords but with words. Fierce debates about the nature of God were raging. The combatants were ministers of the Congregational Church. On one side were the orthodox ministers, and on the other, the liberals.

Orthodox ministers held fast to the traditional Calvinist beliefs that the Puritans brought to American shores. One of their teachings was that every person would suffer for eternity in the fires of hell if God did not choose to save their souls. "In Adam's fall, we sinned all" was the first sentence most children learned to read in their schoolbooks, reflecting the notion that all people are inherently sinful and by nature unworthy to go to heaven after death. Orthodox ministers constantly reminded their congregations that they were miserable sinners, despicable in the sight of God. They also preached that God had already decided the fate of every person. You couldn't go to heaven unless you were one of God's elect. But how could you know if you were chosen? You had to experience an intense moment of revelation and repentance that assured you of God's grace. If you failed to have such an experience, known as a conversion, you were doomed. The sermons of the orthodox ministers were filled with dramatic images that stirred the emotions and inspired fear and awe.

The liberal ministers had a different point of view. They believed in the power of reason and did not trust emotional appeals. They studied the Christian Bible and found that it did not support the doctrines of Calvinist orthodoxy. In their view, every person had the power to choose goodness over sin. People could redeem themselves by living virtuous lives. They believed that God had given people the powers of reason and conscience so that they could choose right over wrong. Liberal ministers were likely to preach about duty and personal responsibility rather than fear and repentance. They did not directly challenge the old Calvinist doctrines, but they avoided mentioning the points they disagreed with. The God they believed in was a loving father and not the unyielding tyrant of Calvinist faith.

As the war of words raged, another important disagreement surfaced. The liberal ministers rejected the Trinity, the idea that

God has three aspects: Father, Son, and Holy Spirit. Their insistence that God is one outraged the orthodox ministers and gave them ammunition for angry denunciations. A minister named Jedidiah Morse published an article that accused the liberal ministers of believing exactly what English Unitarians believed and of using hypocrisy and deception to hide their true beliefs.

William Ellery Channing, the minister of the Federal Street Church in Boston, was a man who hated controversy. He had always been tolerant of other people's beliefs, and he expected them to return the courtesy. But the one thing Channing valued above all was his integrity. When Morse made false claims about his beliefs, and—even worse!—accused Channing and his associates of not being honest about what they believed, Channing felt compelled to respond. He refuted Morse's "false and injurious charges" by clearly laying out the position of the liberal ministers. In so doing, he officially joined the fray.

Although Channing had been something of a moderate when the war of words began to heat up in 1805, his beliefs gradually moved to the liberal side. He was a beloved minister, an eloquent speaker, and a persuasive writer. Now he was becoming the leading spokesperson for the liberal movement.

The event that fanned the flames of controversy to such a fury in 1805 was the appointment of a liberal minister to the most important position in theology at Harvard College, where most Massachusetts ministers, liberal and orthodox, were educated. The orthodox ministers were horrified by the liberal takeover of the school and soon established a competing seminary in Andover. They refused to exchange pulpits with liberal ministers anymore, a practice that up to that time had been common.

Orthodox members of churches that chose liberal ministers began splitting away to form their own congregations. Even as the liberal ministers continued to campaign for peace and unity, it became increasingly clear that the split within the Congregational Church could not be mended. The time had come for the liberals to state their position once and for all and to give it a name.

The moment chosen for this declaration was May 5, 1819. A young minister named Jared Sparks was to be ordained as minister of a newly formed liberal church in Baltimore, Maryland. William Ellery Channing was chosen to deliver the sermon. His words that day were a carefully crafted statement of beliefs that he called "Unitarian Christianity." The sermon was a huge success and was immediately published as a pamphlet that gained immense popularity. Thousands and thousands of copies were printed and read between 1819 and 1824.

From that time on, many congregations called themselves Unitarian, especially in eastern Massachusetts. Members of the Unitarian churches often included the community's most prominent leaders in business, the professions, and the arts. Nonetheless, American Unitarianism had trouble becoming an established denomination. Many of the ministers, including Channing, were completely opposed to forming a new sect. They had fought for the right to think freely, and they did not want to bind themselves, or anyone else, to a new orthodoxy. They formed the American Unitarian Association in 1825, but gave it little support.

Gradually, a new split developed. There were Unitarians who, like Channing, firmly believed that each person must follow his own thought. There were others who believed that certain core Unitarian beliefs must be defended. They wrestled with how a body founded on the principle of free thought could define the limits of freedom.

In 1841, the Unitarians were forced to face that question squarely. A charismatic Unitarian minister named Theodore Parker delivered a sermon in which he suggested that the miracles of the Bible were not factually true. In the uproar that followed the sermon, most Unitarian ministers agreed that Parker had gone too far. They said that he could no longer be considered a Christian, and they challenged him, hoping that he would resign from the ministry. Parker defended his beliefs and refused to resign. Channing defended Parker's right to remain. Even though he disagreed with Theodore Parker about the miracles, he was convinced that

Parker was an honest seeker of truth. In the end, Channing's spirit of open-mindedness prevailed, and Parker continued to preach.

William Ellery Channing once said that nothing discouraged him more than people who were "looking out for some beaten path." He believed that each of us must find the truth for ourselves and not adopt some other person's thought. This confidence in the ability of people to think for themselves is an important part of what Unitarian Universalists still believe today. We can thank Channing for planting the seeds of free thought that have grown into our open-minded Unitarian Universalist faith.

Quotations for Discussion

In 1815, Channing chided the orthodox ministers for appointing themselves as judges of the liberal ministers, saying,

> Men differ in opinion as much as in features. No two minds are perfectly accordant. The shades of belief are infinitely diversified. Amidst the immense variety of sentiment, every man is right in his own eyes. Every man discovers errors in the creed of his brother. Every man is prone to magnify the importance of his own peculiarities, and to discover danger in the peculiarities of others. This is human nature.

In her *Reminiscences of Rev. Wm. Ellery Channing, D.D.*, Elizabeth Palmer Peabody wrote,

> I largely owe to him the salutary conviction that nobody believes what is false because it is false, but because it seems to be true; and that we can best set guards against our own narrowness and prevent the spirit of the Pharisee in our own hearts by tenderly inquiring into the mental history of our opponent, to learn how what appears false to us can seem true to him. For we grow in universality by respecting individuals, and so help to make mankind as a whole the image

of God, without losing personal life in a vague spirituality, abhorrent to "the human heart by which we live."

Discussion: How is Channing's support for diversity of theological belief manifested in our congregations today? How do we fall short of Channing's ideal? What are the theological orthodoxies in contemporary Unitarian Universalism? What are the social orthodoxies?

In his 1830 Election Day sermon, Channing asserts,

> I call that mind free which jealously guards its intellectual rights and powers, which calls no man master, which does not content itself with a passive or hereditary faith, which opens itself to light whencesoever it may come, which receives new truth as an angel from heaven, which, while consulting others, inquires still more of the oracle within itself.

Discussion: Receiving new truth with an open mind can be both rewarding and challenging. What experiences have you had that caused you to see a "new truth"?

This passage, from a talk by Channing to the Sunday-School Society, can be found in *Singing the Living Tradition* and is often quoted in sermons or brochures about children's religious education and faith development:

> The great end in religious instruction is not to stamp our
>   minds upon the young, but to stir up their own;
> Not to make them see with our eyes, but to look inquir-
>   ingly and steadily with their own;

Not to give them a definite amount of knowledge, but to inspire a fervent love of truth;
Not to form an outward regularity, but to touch inward springs;
Not to bind them by ineradicable prejudices to our particular sect or peculiar notions,
but to prepare them for impartial, conscientious judging of whatever subjects may be offered to their decision;
Not to burden the memory, but to quicken and strengthen the power of thought;
Not to impose religion upon them in the form of arbitrary rules, but to awaken the conscience, the moral discernment.

Discussion: How does this statement remain current nearly two hundred years after it was written?

⑥

Channing preached a sermon in 1828 called "Humanity's Likeness to God." It anticipates the Transcendentalist view that the human spirit is inherently divine. He ends the sermon with these words:

The Infinite Light would be forever hidden from us, did not kindred rays dawn and brighten within us. God is another name for human intelligence, raised above all error and imperfection, and extended to all possible truth.

Discussion: In what ways is Channing's definition of God similar to your own understanding? How does it differ? What implications does Channing's understanding of God have for the contemporary Unitarian Universalist quest to build multicultural, multigenerational communities? Are there ways in which Channing's words support that vision? Are there ways in which Channing's ideas impede the realization of that vision?

Connecting with Our Lives

In Our Faith Communities
In a small group or a broader congregational conversation, consider the challenges Unitarian Universalists embrace as part of a community where one of the principal commitments the group holds is freedom of thought. Encourage them to discuss what holds a Unitarian Universalist congregation together and what is at the core of Unitarian Universalist identity.

Invite members of your faith community to attend children's worship or volunteer to work with a children's group in the congregation. Encourage the volunteers to explore how the religious education program reflects Channing's ideal of "inspiring a fervent love of truth" and "touching inward springs." Ask them to help plan a special event for the children with Channing's idea in mind.

If you are in a Coming of Age group or are a Coming of Age mentor, consider how your relationship with your mentor or mentee reflects Channing's ideal of religious education. Together, determine whether your conversations and activities serve to "stir up" each others' minds or "awaken the conscience, the moral discernment" in each other. Find an activity—someplace or someone to visit, a volunteer project, something to read or watch and discuss, a new skill to learn—that you think will "touch inner springs" in both mentee and mentor.

At Home
Talk with your family about ideas or values you would be willing to defend, even though you know that many friends and neighbors are likely to disagree.

What does the idea that "God is one" mean to you? Make a drawing, painting, or other piece of art (visual or otherwise) based on this or another of Channing's ideas. If you want to work with a group, you could create a large painting or mural inspired by the idea of the oneness of God or any of Channing's other ideas.

Find Out More

Buell, Lawrence. *The American Transcendentalists: Essential Writings.* New York: Modern Library, 2006.

Carpenter, Frank. "William Ellery Channing." *Dictionary of Unitarian and Universalist Biography*, published online by the Unitarian Universalist Historical Society at www25.uua.org/uuhs.

Chadwick, John White. *William Ellery Channing: Minister of Religion.* Boston: Riverside Press, 1903. It can be read online at Google Books.

Mendelsohn, Jack. *Channing, the Reluctant Radical.* Boston: Little, Brown, 1971.

Peabody, Elizabeth Palmer. *Reminiscences of Rev. Wm. Ellery Channing, D.D.* Boston: Roberts Brothers, 1880. It can be read online at Google Books.

Wright, Conrad. *Three Prophets of Religious Liberalism: Channing, Emerson, Parker.* 2nd ed. Boston: Skinner House, 1986.

Texts of Channing's works can be found on the American Unitarian Conference website at www.americanunitarian.org/channing.htm.

Ralph Waldo Emerson and the Birth of Transcendentalism

In 1828, William Ellery Channing declared, "The idea of God . . . is the idea of our own spiritual nature, purified and enlarged to infinity. In ourselves are the elements of the Divinity." This sermon, known as "Likeness to God," contained the seeds of a new movement that began within the Unitarian Church in the 1830s—a movement that came to be known as American Transcendentalism. The leaders of the movement looked to Channing as their mentor, but they were ready to take liberal religious thought in new directions that departed from his beliefs.

The movement began with a group of young Unitarian ministers who had become dissatisfied with the chilly and unemotional atmosphere at the core of Unitarianism. The Unitarians of Channing's generation had a tendency to insist that the fundamental way of knowing God is through reason. It seemed to a number of the next generation that this intellectual approach to religion robbed it of its spiritual nature. They began to move in a direction that emphasized the intuitive, mysterious, spontaneous nature of spiritual knowing. Ralph Waldo Emerson (1803–1882), Transcendentalism's most prominent spokesperson, led the way.

Because the Transcendentalists believed that God is within each individual and that connection with God can be achieved intuitively without the assistance of any formal religion, it is not surprising that some of them broke their official tie to Unitarianism altogether. Nonetheless, the Transcendentalist thinkers influenced the currents of religious thought in America, both inside and outside the Unitarian Church.

In 1829, at the age of twenty-six, Ralph Waldo Emerson became minister of the Second Church of Boston. It was a plum position for a young minister, and he was well liked by his congregation. Why then, less than four years later, did he resign his pulpit? He could no longer in good conscience serve the Lord's Supper, he explained. He no longer wished to observe the sacrament of Communion with bread and wine. Emerson carefully laid out his reasons, hoping he might persuade his congregation to give up the practice. But as much as they liked their pastor and wished him to stay, they would not agree to abandon this important ritual of Christian faith.

Perhaps Emerson chose to precipitate this crisis in his career because a part of him knew it was time to move on. In truth, his discomfort with the Lord's Supper was only one example of his growing unease. The men of his family had been ministers for many generations, and he had long planned to enter the ministry himself. Now he felt very uncertain of his calling. He was a free thinker who hated to stay within the confines of prescribed beliefs and practices. He was perpetually questioning and re-examining, perpetually searching for truth. The only part of being a minister that he was sure he liked was preaching. He was tired of attending to church business and making pastoral visits. He was tired of the dry theology of the Unitarians. And at the same time, he was feeling a profound emptiness in his personal life. His young wife Ellen, the love of his life, had died of tuberculosis after less than two years of marriage.

Something inside him made him leave parish ministry and turn his face toward an unknown future. On Christmas day, he set out alone on a ship headed for Europe. He had no specific plan except to explore his life and its meaning. He began in Italy, and then traveled to Paris, England, and Scotland, all the while carefully recording his thoughts and experiences in a journal.

After nine months abroad, Emerson returned to Massachusetts with no clear direction but with the sense that he had hit bottom and was ready to climb back up. To earn a living, he substituted in pulpits that needed a temporary preacher, and meanwhile, he wrote. Ever since his teenage years, Emerson had been keeping a journal, intending to use it as a resource for his poems and essays. Now he used the ideas he had been developing over the years to create his first book, a slender volume called *Nature* that he published early in 1836. The book was a long poetical essay exploring his beliefs about the role of nature in revealing God to humankind. The following year, he delivered an address called "The American Scholar" to the Phi Beta Kappa Society at Harvard. These two achievements helped set Emerson on course for a new career as a writer and lecturer.

At the beginning of *Nature*, Emerson writes, "The foregoing generations beheld God and nature face to face; we—, through their eyes. Why should not we also enjoy an original relation to the universe? Why should not we have a poetry and philosophy of insight and not of tradition, and a religion by revelation to us, and not the history of theirs?" The idea he was expressing—that we should experience God and nature directly, in the present, and not depend on secondhand experiences or traditions from the past—is central to Emerson's beliefs. In "The American Scholar," he expresses this theme again. The scholar, he says, is not a person who parrots other people's thinking, but one whose own original thought arises from the study of nature and from personal experiences and actions, as well as from books. Self-trust is key. The ideal scholar "believes himself inspired by the Divine Soul which also inspires all men."

Emerson hoped to steer people away from their conventional, well-worn paths into new ways of thinking. He was not alone in his search for fresh ideas. Shortly after *Nature* appeared, he and a group of friends, mostly dissatisfied young Unitarian ministers, decided to establish a forum for discussing new viewpoints on religion and society. The group had a variety of different names, but it gradually came to be known as the Transcendental Club. The group met about thirty times between 1836 and 1840. Membership grew to include many of the most progressive thinkers of the day, among them George Ripley, Bronson Alcott, Elizabeth Peabody, Margaret Fuller, James Freeman Clarke, and Henry David Thoreau. Because it was founded on a principle of free and open discussion, the group subscribed to no particular set of beliefs, but members did share some common ground. They all agreed that individuals should strive for self-improvement, and they were interested in exploring new ways to improve society. They believed that the divine spirit is present in the human soul and in nature and that a person can discover truth and morality through intuition. They were open to new ideas coming out of Europe, and they were interested in other religious traditions, such as Hinduism and classical mythology.

Of the ministers in the Transcendental group, ten remained in Unitarian pulpits. Others, like Emerson, went off in new directions. In 1838, Emerson was invited by graduating seniors to give an address at Harvard Divinity School. He used that occasion to criticize the Unitarian ministry of the day, taking aim at the major tenets of Unitarian theology, and he urged the young ministers to preach from their hearts and from the truth of their own lives.

Needless to say, Emerson's "Divinity School Address" deeply offended and angered the Unitarian faculty at Harvard. He was not invited to speak there again for nearly thirty years. Fortunately, there was a popular new adult education movement in America called the lyceum. Lyceums were local associations that sponsored lectures and debates on various topics of current interest, and there were about three thousand of them in the Northeast and the Midwest. Ralph Waldo Emerson became one of the most popular speakers on the circuit. People loved to hear him speak, even when they had little idea what he was talking about in his rambling poetical discourses. Emerson's lecturing career gave him the opportunity to develop his ideas and spread them widely. It also allowed him to support a family. In 1835, Emerson bought a house in Concord, Massachusetts, which soon became a hub for visits, conversations, and discussions among a wide variety of thinkers and reformers. He married Lydia Jackson that same year, and they had four children.

Emerson remained friends with members of the Transcendental Club all his life, but the group stopped meeting as their priorities began to diverge. Although members of the club viewed perfecting themselves and perfecting society as intertwined pursuits, some, like Emerson, focused primarily on spiritual concerns and the perfection of the individual. Others turned more of their energies to reforming society.

It is impossible to measure how much impact Ralph Waldo Emerson and his friends had on American life and religious thought. Their influence flowed out into society as circles flow outward from a pebble dropped into a lake. They inspired many people in their own time. Their words and ideas continue to inspire us today.

Quotations for Discussion

In his "Divinity School Address" (1838), Emerson took aim at two major tenets of the Unitarian theology of the day: the argument that Jesus' miracles proved the authenticity of Christianity and the idea that Jesus was God's only messenger on earth.

Here are some of the words he said that day:

> Historical Christianity has fallen into the error that corrupts all attempts to communicate religion.... It dwells with noxious exaggeration about the person of Jesus. The soul knows no persons. It invites every man to expand to the full circle of the universe....
>
> In how many churches, by how many prophets, tell me, is man made sensible that he is an infinite Soul; that the earth and heavens are passing into his mind; that he is drinking forever the soul of God?

Discussion: Have you ever had a mystical experience that allowed you to "expand to the full circle of the universe"? What was your experience? How might Emerson respond to contemporary calls for deeper spiritual experience in Unitarian Universalist congregational life?

☙

From "Circles" (1841) by Ralph Waldo Emerson:

> Our life is an apprenticeship to the truth that around every circle another can be drawn; that there is no end in nature, but every end is a beginning; that there is always another dawn risen on mid-noon, and under every deep a lower deep opens.
>
> In nature every moment is new; the past is always swallowed and forgotten; the coming only is sacred. Nothing is secure but life, transition, the energizing spirit. No love can be bound by oath or covenant to secure it against a higher love. No truth so sublime but it may be trivial to-morrow in the light of new thoughts. People wish to be settled; only as far as they are unsettled is there any hope for them.

Discussion: Do you ever long to be "settled"? How do you respond to Emerson's idea that it is only in being "unsettled" that there is hope? How does contemporary Unitarian Universalism reflect Emerson's love of the new? What do you perceive as shortcomings in Emerson's point of view?

☙

The American poet Walt Whitman (1819–1892) was much inspired by the writings of Ralph Waldo Emerson. "I was simmering, simmering, simmering," he said, "and Emerson brought me to a boil." His poem "Miracles" echoes the Transcendentalist viewpoint in the debate that raged among Unitarians over the meaning of miracles:

Why, who makes much of a miracle?
As to me I know of nothing else but miracles,
Whether I walk the streets of Manhattan,
Or dart my sight over the roofs of houses toward the sky,
Or wade with naked feet along the beach just in the edge of the water,
Or stand under trees in the woods,
Or talk by day with any one I love, or sleep in the bed at night with any one I love,
Or sit at table at dinner with the rest,
Or look at strangers opposite me riding in the car,
Or watch honey-bees busy around the hive of a summer forenoon,
Or animals feeding in the fields,
Or birds, or the wonderfulness of insects in the air,
Or the wonderfulness of the sundown, or of stars shining so quiet and bright,
Or the exquisite delicate thin curve of the new moon in spring;
These with the rest, one and all, are to me miracles,
The whole referring, yet each distinct and in its place.

To me every hour of the light and dark is a miracle,
Every cubic inch of space is a miracle,
Every square yard of the surface of the earth is spread with the same,
Every foot of the interior swarms with the same.
To me the sea is a continual miracle,
The fishes that swim—the rocks—the motion of the waves—the ships with men in them,
What stranger miracles are there?

Discussion: What in Whitman's poem and the Transcendentalist understanding of miracles speaks to you?

From "The Over-Soul" (1841) by Ralph Waldo Emerson:

> The Supreme Critic on the errors of the past and the present, and the only prophet of that which must be, is that great nature in which we rest, as the earth lies in the soft arms of the atmosphere; that Unity, that Over-soul, within which every man's particular being is contained and made one with all other; that common heart, of which all sincere conversation is the worship, to which all right action is submission; that overpowering reality which confutes our tricks and talents, and constrains every one to pass for what he is, and to speak from his character, and not from his tongue, and which evermore tends to pass into our thought and hand, and become wisdom, and virtue, and power, and beauty. We live in succession, in division, in parts, in particles. Meantime within man is the soul of the whole; the wise silence; the universal beauty, to which every part and particle is equally related; the eternal ONE. And this deep power in which we exist, and whose beatitude is all accessible to us, is not only self-sufficing and perfect in every hour, but the act of seeing and the thing seen, the seer and the spectacle, the subject and the object, are one. We see the world piece by piece, as the sun, the moon, the animal, the tree; but the whole, of which these are the shining parts, is the soul.

Discussion: What in Emerson's description of the eternal ONE reflects your own spiritual experiences?

From "Self-Reliance" (1841) by Ralph Waldo Emerson:

> A foolish consistency is the hobgoblin of little minds, adored by little statesmen and philosophers and divines. With con-

sistency a great soul has simply nothing to do. He may as well concern himself with his shadow on the wall. Speak what you think now and in hard words, and to-morrow speak what to-morrow thinks in hard words again, though it contradict every thing you said to-day.—"Ah, so you shall be sure to be misunderstood."—Is it so bad then, to be misunderstood?

Discussion: How do you respond to this famous quote? How is Emerson's unshakeable faith in the future, in new ideas and new understanding, manifested in contemporary Unitarian Universalism? What wisdom does this approach offer for your own life?

Connecting with Our Lives

In Our Faith Communities
Invite members of your faith community to share images or words that they use to describe the creative force of the universe. Sharing might be done via an art activity or a conversation, and might be part of a worship service or small group experience. Note that Emerson himself turned to the Quaker image of inner light and the Hindu understanding of Brahman to help him describe this force. Emerson variously called this timeless entity "the essential oneness of all things," the "Over-Soul," the "Unity," the "eternal ONE," "that great nature in which we rest," "that common heart," and the "wise silence."

Invite members of your faith community to map their own spiritual journeys, using art materials to create a visual representation of the journey. Encourage them to reflect on what they have embraced, what they have rejected, and which events and people have helped them grow in understanding, in wisdom, and in spirit. Invite them to consider times when they, like Emerson, intentionally sought knowledge and wisdom, and times when their spiritual wisdom grew as a result of life experiences. With permission from their creators, display the faith journey maps and invite others in the congregation to try the same exercise.

At Home
Emerson's journal played an important part in his life and his thinking. He kept the kind of journal called a "commonplace book." A commonplace book is a place to collect your thoughts about your encounters with people, books, events, what you have watched or listened to; it is also a place to collect passages or poems from your reading that are particularly important or memorable. Do you or other family members currently keep a journal or commonplace book? Try creating a family commonplace book in which each person contributes favorite quotes, poems, and memories to make a family compendium.

Find Out More

Andrews, Barry M. *Emerson as Spiritual Guide*. Boston: Skinner House, 2003.

Buell, Lawrence. *The American Transcendentalists: Essential Writings*. New York: Modern Library, 2006.

Gura, Philip F. *American Transcendentalism: A History*. New York: Hill and Wang, 2007.

Richardson, Robert D., Jr. *Emerson: The Mind on Fire*. Berkeley: University of California Press, 1995.

Schulman, Frank. "Ralph Waldo Emerson." *Dictionary of Unitarian and Universalist Biography*, published online by the Unitarian Universalist Historical Society at www25.uua.org/uuhs.

Wright, Conrad. T*hree Prophets of Religious Liberalism: Channing, Emerson, Parker*. 2nd ed. Boston: Skinner House, 1986.

The text of Emerson's original works can be found on The Works of Ralph Waldo Emerson website at www.rwe.org.

Henry David Thoreau's Search for Higher Truth

In his essay "Self-Reliance," Ralph Waldo Emerson asserts, "Whoso would be a man must be a nonconformist." Emerson tended to find friends who fit this description. Not long after purchasing a house in Concord, Massachusetts, Emerson became friends with a native of the town who fit his ideal remarkably well. The young man had just finished college at the time. His name was Henry David Thoreau.

Henry Thoreau had roots in Concord's Unitarian Church, where he was baptized in 1817 and where his funeral was held in 1862. But as a young man, Thoreau renounced his church membership. He had an aversion to institutions and all his life avoided membership in any organization that might encourage conformity of thought. Even among the Transcendentalists, Thoreau stood out as perhaps the ultimate nonconformist. He lived by his ideals and didn't seek to please others. He was a serious scholar with an inventive mind who was also good at working with his hands. No one more faithfully lived by the Transcendentalist ideal of individual self-improvement. No one more faithfully strove to maintain a direct, intuitive relationship to the divine.

Although Henry David Thoreau was not widely known in his own day, he has become the best known and best loved of the Transcendentalist writers. We associate him most closely, perhaps, with social justice and environmentalism. His essay "Civil Disobedience" inspired the twentieth-century nonviolent resistance movements of Gandhi and Martin Luther King Jr. His nature writing, with its early insight into the value of wilderness and the costs of an overly materialistic culture, continues to inspire environmentalists today. This story takes a look at the man himself, focusing on the spirituality at the heart of his writing—on his devotion to finding the sacred in the everyday and his aspiration to touch eternity in every moment.

[A note on the pronunciation of Thoreau's name: Although most Americans today emphasize the second syllable, it can be inferred from a number of sources that Thoreau himself put the accent on the first syllable, making a pun of the slogan "I do a thorough job."]

In 1837, when Henry Thoreau was graduating from Harvard College, he gave a speech called "The Commercial Spirit of Modern Times." It rang out, not with the values of the business community, but with his own rebellious spirit. He turned the Bible story of six days of work followed by a Sabbath day of rest on its head, suggesting that just one day should be for earning a living by the sweat of the brow, while the other six should be our Sabbath of the soul—a time in which to drink in "the soft influences and sublime revelations of nature."

Working just one day a week and spending the other six drinking in the sublime revelations of nature? Surely no one could take such an idea seriously. The young Henry Thoreau may have been exaggerating for effect; yet to the end of his life, he never quite gave up on the idea. Conventional jobs would never appeal to him. Working for money would never completely distract him from a calling that pulled him in other directions. "The cost of a thing is the amount of what I call life which is required to be exchanged for it, immediately or in the long run," he wrote. He was determined to keep his costs down.

As a boy growing up in Concord, Massachusetts, Henry spent much of his time exploring the town's woods and fields and rivers. He was a keen observer of nature and something of a loner, although he was seldom alone. He lived with his parents, sisters, brother, and aunts; and, since his mother kept a boardinghouse, there were usually assorted others in the house as well.

When Henry came home from college in 1837, he visited Ralph Waldo Emerson, who had recently moved to Concord. The previous year, Emerson had published a book called *Nature*. Henry Thoreau had read the book and found that it matched his own way of thinking exactly. Emerson was fourteen years older than Thoreau, but their ideas about life were so compatible that the two men soon became close friends.

To make a living, Thoreau took on various teaching jobs and helped out in his father's pencil-making business. He developed new manufacturing techniques that made Thoreau pencils the very best pencils made in America. But he did not wish to devote his life to the business of pencil making. To him it seemed that most people lived lives of "quiet desperation." He saw that "In the long run men hit only what they aim at," and he was determined to aim high.

In 1841, he accepted the invitation of Emerson and his wife to live with them as a general handyman and family friend. This gave him access to the books in Emerson's library and to the many intellectuals, free thinkers, and disciples who came to the Emersons' home for conversation and inspiration. It was an excellent launching pad for a young man on a spiritual quest—a man whose heart was set on a career as a poet, a philosopher, and a seeker.

Thoreau began keeping a journal when he returned to Concord, and it was around this time that he renounced his membership in Concord's Unitarian Church. In those days, Unitarian faith focused quite narrowly on the Christian Bible. In his search for what he called the Higher Truth, Thoreau ranged far more widely. He found his greatest inspiration in the natural world and in the sacred texts of India and ancient Greece.

Henry Thoreau was very close to his brother John. For a while they had run a school together, and in 1839, they had made a journey up the Concord and Merrimack rivers into New Hampshire in a boat they had built themselves. In 1842, John contracted tetanus, and Henry rushed to his side. As his brother watched over him, John died a painful death. Henry was so deeply affected that he became ill himself. Then, only a few days later, Emerson's beloved five-year-old son Waldo died of scarlet fever. In the months and years that followed, both men struggled to come through their grief with a deeper understanding of life's meaning.

Thoreau had long yearned for a chance to live independently, to lead a quiet life on his own in close communion with nature. Now his friendship with Emerson gave him the opportunity to realize his dream. Emerson bought some land bordering a beautiful little lake called Walden Pond. Within easy walking distance of Emerson's house, it was a secluded and peaceful spot. The two men agreed that Thoreau should live there.

Thoreau built a small cabin in the woods beside the lake and moved in on July 4, 1845. "I went to the woods because I wished to live deliberately," he writes, "to front only the essential facts of life, and see if I could not learn what it had to teach." He was eager "to stand on the meeting of two eternities, the past and future, which is precisely the present moment."

For Thoreau, life at Walden Pond was a happy interweaving of the active and the contemplative life. He enjoyed long hours of solitude, but he also had ample opportunities to walk into town or to entertain visitors at his cabin. He planted a bean field, cut wood, took long walks, read scholarly books, and wrote and wrote and wrote.

Thoreau's writing tells about his everyday experiences, but from each experience, he draws deeper meanings. Outward reality is a pathway for the inner journey. Don't just explore the world, he urges his readers, but "be a Columbus to whole new continents and worlds within you, opening new channels, not of trade, but of thought." Morning symbolized for Thoreau the awakened mind. The cycle of the seasons represented the eternal promise of rebirth and renewal. At Walden Pond, Thoreau felt fully alive and awake to the world. He found peace in the certainty of eternal change.

After living at Walden for two years, two months, and two days, Thoreau moved out of his little house. While there, he had completed the first draft of a book about the river trip he had taken with John, and he had filled many notebooks with thoughts and observations that would later become his second and most famous book, *Walden*. "I left the woods for as good a reason as I went there," he wrote. "Perhaps it seemed to me that I had several more lives to live, and could not spare any more time for that one."

Thoreau continued to observe nature in and around Concord. He became a skillful land-surveyor, although surveying was not so much a calling as a convenient way to earn a living while getting to know every nook and cranny and contour of the town. His observations of nature were astonishingly detailed and precise. He knew every plant and animal, every insect, bird, and fish. Scientists today still find his records useful. But Thoreau did not see himself as a scientist. In 1853, when asked to fill out a form for possible membership in the Association for the Advancement of Science, he chose not to describe the branch of science that specially interested him. It would make him a laughingstock of the scientific community, he said, for "the fact is I am a mystic, a transcendentalist, and a natural philosopher to boot."

He knew that to most people his vocation seemed eccentric and even ridiculous. He poked fun at it himself, saying that he was the "self-appointed inspector of snow-storms" and "a reporter to a journal of no very wide circulation." He took pleasure in boasting, "I have traveled a good deal—in Concord."

But in fact, this comment was not just a joke. Knowing one place well, he believed, is a key to unlocking the deepest mysteries of creation. If you give reality your full attention—seeing it clearly and reflecting on it deeply—it will reveal the eternal laws of the universe. The only place to find reality is where you are. The only time to do it is now. And you must be fully aware: "Only that day dawns to which we are awake."

Quotations for Discussion

Thoreau often wrote about time and eternity. The first two paragraphs below are from the chapter "Where I Lived and What I Lived For" in *Walden*, and the third is from a journal entry dated April 24, 1859:

Men esteem truth remote, in the outskirts of the system, behind the farthest star, before Adam and after the last man. In eternity there is indeed something true and sublime. But all these times and places and occasions are now and here. God himself culminates in the present moment, and will never be more divine in the lapse of all the ages. And we are enabled to apprehend at all what is sublime and noble only by the perpetual instilling and drenching of the reality that surrounds us. . . .

Time is but the stream I go a-fishing in. I drink at it; but while I drink I see the sandy bottom and detect how shallow it is. Its thin current slides away, but eternity remains. I would drink deeper; fish in the sky, whose bottom is pebbly with stars.

We must not be governed by rigid rules, as by the almanac, but let the season rule us. The moods and thoughts of man are revolving just as steadily and incessantly as nature's. Nothing must be postponed. Take time by the forelock. Now or never! You must live in the present, launch yourself on every wave, find your eternity in each moment. Fools stand on their island opportunities and look toward another land. There is no other land; there is no other life but this.

Discussion: What role or roles does "time" play in your life? Does your understanding of time have a spiritual dimension? What wisdom do Thoreau's observations offer that is applicable in your own life?

Friends who wrote about Thoreau after his death often emphasized his extraordinary relationship to the natural world and his somewhat less comfortable relationship to human society. The following quotes from Bronson Alcott (1799–1888) and Ralph Waldo Emerson (1803–1888) illustrate these points:

His senses seemed double, giving him access to secrets not easily read by others; . . . an instinct for seeing and judging, as by some other, or seventh sense; dealing with objects as if they were shooting forth from his mind mythologically. . . . I am sure he knew the animals one by one. . . ; the plants, the geography, as Adam did in his Paradise. . . .
The world was holy, the things seen symbolizing the things unseen, and thus worthy of worship, calling men out-of-doors and under the firmament for health and wholesomeness to be insinuated into their souls, not as idolators, but as idealists. . . .
His politics were of a piece with his individualism. We must admit that he found little in political or religious establishments answering to his wants.

—Bronson Alcott

He was equally interested in every natural fact. The depth of his perception found likeness of law throughout Nature, and I know not any genius who so swiftly inferred universal law from the single fact. He was not pedant of a department. His eye was open to beauty, and his ear to music. He found these, not in rare conditions, but wheresoever he went.

. . . Whilst he used in his writings a certain petulance of remark in reference to churches or churchmen, he was a person of a rare, tender and absolute religion, a person incapable of any profanation, by act or by thought. Of course, the same isolation which belonged to his original thinking and living detached him from the social religious forms. This is neither to be censured nor regretted. Aristotle long ago explained it, when he said, "One who surpasses his fellow citizens in virtue is no longer a part of the city. Their law is not for him, since he is a law to himself."

—Ralph Waldo Emerson

Discussion: What is appealing to you about Thoreau's way of life? What was missing in Thoreau's way of life that is important to you? How is it that contemporary Unitarian Universalists have so eagerly embraced one who had no need for organized religion?

Many of the most well-known sayings from *Walden* express Thoreau's devotion to self-sufficiency and the integrity of the individual. Here are some examples:

> I learned this, at least, by my experiment; that if one advances confidently in the direction of his dreams, and endeavors to live the life which he has imagined, he will meet with a success unexpected in common hours. . . . In proportion as he simplifies his life, the laws of the universe will appear less complex, and solitude will not be solitude, nor poverty poverty, nor weakness weakness. If you have built castles in the air, your work need not be lost; that is where they should be. Now put the foundations under them.

> Why should we be in such desperate haste to succeed and in such desperate enterprises? If a man does not keep pace with his companions, perhaps it is because he hears a different drummer. Let him step to the music which he hears, however measured or far away.

> My greatest skill has been to want but little.

Discussion: Have you heard or perhaps used these or other quotes from Thoreau? What did they mean to you? How does their meaning change or deepen when viewed in the context of his entire life and work?

Connecting with Our Lives

In Our Faith Communities
Unlike the Unitarian Church of Thoreau's day, Unitarian Universalists today embrace a wide range of sources as inspiration for their faith. Invite members of your faith community to reread the part of the Principles of the Unitarian Universalist Association that describes the sources from which we draw our living tradition. Discuss the extent to which Thoreau drew from these same sources.

Spend some time closely inspecting and appreciating your backyard, a park, or another area close to you. Make a list or map that includes all that you find there: soil types, plant life, rocks, wildlife, and insects, as well as human-made materials. Invite people of all ages in your community to join you in appreciating the natural area you have chosen. Consider extending your attention of the area by undertaking a project that benefits the natural world (e.g., litter clean-up, providing shelter for birds, or planting native species).

At Home
Read and consider the poem "Going to Walden" by Mary Oliver, published in *New and Selected Poems, Volume 1*:

> It isn't very far as highways lie.
> I might be back by night fall, having seen
> The rough pines, and the stones, and the clear water.
> Friends argue that I might be wiser for it.
> They do not hear that far-off Yankee whisper:
> How dull we grow from hurrying here and there!
>
> Many have gone, and think me half a fool
> To miss a day away in the cool country.
> Maybe. But in a book I read and cherish,
> Going to Walden is not so easy a thing
> As a green visit. It is the slow and difficult
> Trick of living, and finding it where you are.

To what extent do we pay attention to the reality of where we live? Do we truly know our own natural environment? Are we aware of the cycles of the days and seasons? Spend some time outdoors as a family, examining the various ecosystems in your own town or city. Pay attention to each kind of weather, each phase of the moon, the sounds and the silences around you.

Thoreau said that instead of working six days a week with one day of rest, perhaps we should work one day a week and leave the other six to appreciate "the soft influences and sublime revelations of nature." Try observing the Sabbath by taking one entire day to contemplate and meditate, interacting minimally with the complexities of modern life, such as television, the Internet, and cell phones. Good activities for this day include going for a walk, spending time in nature, reading, creating or appreciating art or poetry, meditation, prayer, and conversing with family and friends.

According to Thoreau, "The cost of a thing is the amount of what I call life which is required to be exchanged for it, immediately or in the long run." He thought people spent too much time earning a living rather than living itself. With your family, consider the cost of some of our material goods as the amount of life that must be exchanged for them. Are there ways in which you and your family can agree to simplify and thereby reduce that cost?

Find Out More

Andrews, Barry M. *Thoreau as Spiritual Guide: A Companion to* Walden *for Personal Reflection and Group Discussion.* Boston: Skinner House, 2000.

Buell, Lawrence. *The American Transcendentalists: Essential Writings.* New York: Modern Library, 2006.

Canby, Henry Seidel. *Thoreau.* Boston: Houghton Mifflin, 1939.

Emerson, Edward Waldo. *Henry Thoreau as Remembered by a Young Friend.* Somerville, MA: Thoreau Foundation, 1968: An unabridged unaltered republication of the original edition published by Houghton Mifflin, 1917. It can be read online at Google Books.

Richardson, Robert D., Jr. *Henry Thoreau: A Life of the Mind*. Berkeley: University of California Press, 1986.

Stern, Philip Van Doren. *The Annotated Walden: Walden; or, Life in the Woods by Henry David Thoreau Together with "Civil Disobedience," a detailed Chronology and Various Pieces about Its Author, the Writing and Publishing of the Book*. New York: Barnes and Noble Books, 1970.

Thoreau, Henry David. *Walden & Other Writings of Henry David Thoreau*, ed. and introd. Brooks Atkinson. New York: Modern Library, 1937.

Judith Sargent Murray and American Universalism

The story of our Universalist roots takes us back to Colonial America, to the time of the Revolutionary War. Decades before William Ellery Channing made his famous declaration of Unitarian Christianity, a small group of Universalist dissenters declared their independence from the established Congregational Church in Gloucester, Massachusetts. In 1779, they formed the Independent Church of Christ—the first Universalist church in America—with John Murray as their minister. Two prominent families of Gloucester, the Sargent family and the Stevens family, had a hand in establishing the new church. Judith Sargent (Stevens) Murray (1751–1820) was the daughter of Winthrop Sargent, a prosperous merchant; wife of sea captain John Stevens; and, after the death of John Stevens, wife of Universalist minister John Murray.

Judith Sargent Murray was a remarkable woman. Eighteenth-century Americans generally considered it improper for a woman to express her opinions publicly, and because most women lacked educational opportunities, few had the skills to do so. Yet from an early age, the young Judith Sargent was an avid reader and "scribbler," with an unquenchable desire to make her mark as a literary figure. Universalism, which she encountered at the age of eighteen, asserted that all humanity was one in spirit and that there were no gender distinctions in the intellect. Her faith in this new religious perspective emboldened her to publish a Universalist catechism—the first Universalist textbook in America—and to publish numerous essays and poems with a strongly feminist slant. In her poems and essays, Murray argued that women should have the same educational opportunities as men and that marriage should not be their only viable career option. The systematic way in which women were denied opportunities, she believed, was irrational, unjust, and harmful to society. Her ideas were radical for her time. Her essay "On the Equality of the Sexes" was written in 1779 and published in Massachusetts Magazine *in 1790, two years before the far better-known feminist manifesto* A Vindication of the Rights of Woman *by British writer Mary Wollstonecraft.*

In addition to her published poems, essays, and plays, Judith Sargent Murray left behind a unique record of her life and times in her letter books: twenty bound volumes into which she carefully copied more than two thousand of the letters she wrote between the ages of fourteen and sixty-seven. Although she had high hopes that these documents would be appreciated by generations to come, they remained lost and unread for more than 160 years. The letter books were rediscovered in 1984, thanks to the perseverance of Unitarian Universalist minister Gordon Gibson. Transcriptions of her handwritten letters provide a unique look at the early history of the Universalist movement in America. They reveal an intriguing eighteenth-century voice that was nearly lost to history.

On November 14, 1774, a young woman named Judith Stevens penned an unusual letter to a man she barely knew.

"My Dear Sir," she wrote,

> If I am not mistaken in the character of the person I have the pleasure to address, it will be most agreeable to him, that I should lay aside all that awe, and reverence, which his unquestionable superiority demands, and approach him with the freedom of a sister, conversing with a brother whom she entirely esteems—I am not much accustomed to writing letters, especially to your sex, but if there be neither male nor female in the Emmanuel you promulgate, we may surely, and with the strictest propriety, mingle souls upon paper—I acknowledge a high sense of obligation to you, Sir, I have been instructed by your scriptural investigations, and I have

a grateful heart—Your revered friend, Mr. Relly, had taught me by his writings, the rudiments of the redeeming plan; but you have enlarged my views, expanded my ideas, dissipated my doubts, and led me to anticipate, and with sublime, and solem [sic] pleasure, the [coming] resurrection.

The letter was addressed to Rev. John Murray, a minister who had recently visited the bustling seaport village of Gloucester, Massachusetts, her hometown. As her letter hints, it was highly irregular for a woman to write to a man in this way. But the young Mrs. Stevens was overflowing with enthusiasm for the new religious beliefs that her family had adopted. She was eager to continue a discussion of those beliefs with the charismatic minister who had left town two days earlier. At a time when her country was about to declare independence from British rule, Judith Stevens, along with a small group of family and friends, was about to declare independence from the authority of New England's Calvinist Church.

The quiet rebellion of Judith's family began in 1769, when a British sailor landed briefly in Gloucester and left behind a book written by a minister named James Relly. Judith's father, a wealthy sea merchant, was intrigued by the book. He and several other prominent members of Gloucester's First Parish Congregational Church formed a study group to read and discuss it. Relly's gospel of universal salvation contrasted sharply with the prevailing Calvinist doctrine of eternal damnation. The Massachusetts clergy in those days taught that all people were born sinners, and most would face eternal punishment after death. Relly argued that this could not be true. He reasoned that if all had sinned in Adam, then all were saved in Christ. Relly's interpretations of scripture were logical. They were comforting. And they made good sense to those who believed in a loving God.

Gloucester's small group of Rellyites, as they called themselves, grew more and more convinced that Relly's ideas were true. Still, they might never have stepped outside the bounds of the First Parish Church had it not been for the arrival of John Murray. Murray had first encountered Relly's ideas in England. He had gone to hear Relly preach, with the idea of formulating arguments to contradict him. To his surprise, he was persuaded by Relly's way of thinking instead. He and his wife both embraced the Universalist faith. Then, Murray's wife and child died, leaving him with insurmountable debts and little reason to remain in England. He left for America in 1770 and became an itinerant minister, traveling up and down the East Coast to spread the Universalist message.

When the Rellyites of Gloucester heard that a traveling minister was preaching the very ideas that so interested them, they invited him to Gloucester. John Murray preached from the pulpit of the First Parish Church on two Sundays in 1774 and met with the Rellyite study group each evening in between. The Rellyites were thrilled by Murray's theatrical and persuasive preaching. They knew he was the minister they wanted. The pulpit at First Parish suddenly became available in 1777, and the Rellyites tried to convince the congregation to hire Murray. When the majority chose another minister, the dissenters decided to strike out on their own. In 1779, they formed the Independent Church of Christ—the first Universalist church in America—with John Murray at the helm. Judith Stevens and her husband, John, were among the sixty-one original members.

Judith and John Stevens had no children of their own, but they became the guardians of two orphaned girls. Judith wrote a catechism to teach her foster daughters the tenets of Universalist faith, and in 1782, at the urging of fellow believers who wanted to use her lessons to teach their children, she took the unusual step of publishing her catechism as a book. She hesitated to do so because she knew it could ruin her reputation. Most people considered it improper for a woman to write for publication, and most people strongly objected to Universalism as well. To shield herself, Stevens published the work anonymously. Yet she wrote a preface that gave many clues to her identity. She had hoped to become a writer ever since she was a little girl, and she did not really want her work to go unnoticed now. But she knew that people would gossip.

"When a Female steps without the Line in which Custom hath circumscribed her," she wrote, "she naturally becomes an Object of Speculation." To ward off criticism, the author asserted that her boldness could be excused because spiritual matters exist beyond "the distinction of male and female."

Once she had successfully stepped over the line to become a published author, Judith Stevens's desire to express herself only increased. In 1784, she published an essay about the importance of education for girls in *The Gentleman and Lady's Town and Country Magazine*. She had always felt handicapped by her lack of a good education—something given to her brothers but not to her. Promoting equal education for girls became her lifetime passion. "It was the mode to confine the female intellect within the narrowest bounds," she wrote, "and by consequence, I was robbed of the aid of education—I shall feel the effects of this irrational deprivation, as long as I shall continue an inhabitant of this world."

The Revolutionary War years badly damaged the fortunes of John Stevens. He fled from his creditors in 1786, hoping to set up a new business in the West Indies, but he died soon after. In 1788, Judith married her longtime mentor and soul mate, John Murray. Her family objected to the match because he was socially beneath them, but she loved her second husband deeply and never regretted it.

John Murray encouraged and supported his wife's writing. She began publishing essays and poems under various pen names, both male and female. Her Universalist beliefs had convinced her that men and women were essentially identical in all but body. The example of her own writing helped to prove it. When she wrote in a male guise, no one would guess that the disembodied voice was female—unless perhaps they noticed a persistent devotion to the theme of women's rights.

Judith Sargent Murray's religious beliefs seem quite conservative today. In contrast, the social ideals that grew out of her faith seem surprisingly modern. Her support for separation of church and state, her respect for the right of all people to express their own opinions without fear of persecution, and her belief in the fundamental oneness of humanity, regardless of race, nationality, or gender, put her at the forefront of liberal thought. Judith Sargent Murray was a woman ahead of her time. Universalism was her guiding light.

Quotations for Discussion

The full title of Judith Sargent Murray's Universalist catechism was *Some Deductions from the System Promulgated in the Page of Divine Revelation: Ranged in the Order and Form of a Catechism Intended as an Assistant to the Christian Parent or Teacher*. Catechisms are written in the form of questions and answers. Usually, questions are put to the children, and they are expected to memorize and recite the answers. Murray reversed this, having the child ask questions, thinking this was truer to the way that children actually learn. Here is an example of such an exchange, from a discussion of the nature of God:

> Q. But what idea (give me leave to ask) ought I to form of a Being whom I have never seen?
>
> A. The Deity is invisible, incomprehensible; it is impossible, my dear, for a finite being to form an idea of infinite perfection.
>
> Q. How then can I judge of his power, love, or tenderness?
>
> A. If, upon a return from any of your little visiting excursions, you should behold some beautiful addition to your apparel, or some advantageous alteration in the disposition of the furniture of your chamber, you would take it for granted the hand of affection had been employed, though you was not a spectator of its beneficent operations: So, when you behold the effects, of love, manifested in rain, sun-shine, seed time and harvest, you ought to conclude there is a power divine, though to you invisible; and further, that that power is all good, all gracious, and all mighty.

Discussion: Murray's catechism begins with a child's questions about God and responds to those questions by inviting the child to reflect on experiences of wonder and awe in the natural world. In what ways has your faith journey proceeded from your own questions about humanity, about God, and about the mysteries of life itself?

⚛

Judith Sargent Murray's first essay, published under the pen name Constantia in 1784, argued the case for self-esteem. It was called "Desultory Thoughts upon the Utility of encouraging a degree of Self-Complacency, especially in Female Bosoms." In her original draft, she gave it the succinct title "Reverence Thy Self." The essay begins with the following words:

> I think, to teach young minds to aspire, ought to be the ground work of education: many a laudable achievement is lost, from a persuasion that our efforts are unequal to the arduous attainment. Ambition is a noble principle, which properly directed, may be productive of the most valuable consequences.

The essay argues that girls are too often taught to view themselves as inferior, and proposes that as a parent she would tell her daughter that "you must learn 'to reverence yourself,' that is, your intellectual existence; you must join my efforts, in endeavouring to adorn your mind, for, it is from the proper furnishing of that, you will become indeed a valuable person."

She concludes,

> I am, from observation, persuaded, that many have suffered materially all their life long, from a depression of soul, early inculcated, in compliance to a false maxim, which hath supposed pride would thereby be eradicated. I know there is a contrary extreme, and I would, in almost all cases, prefer the happy medium.

Discussion: What Murray calls "reverencing thyself," we might today call self-esteem. To what degree are Murray's observations about women suffering from a lack of self-esteem valid in our own day? How has concern for self-esteem influenced parenting and educational practices?

⑥

Again using the pen name Constantia, Judith Sargent Murray published "On the Equality of the Sexes" in two installments in the *Massachusetts Magazine* in March and April 1790. The following are excerpts from that work:

> Yet it may be questioned, from what doth this superiority, in this determining faculty of the soul, proceed. May we not trace its source in the difference of education, and continued advantages? Will it be said that the judgment of a male of two years old, is more sage than that of a female's of the same age? I believe the reverse is generally observed to be true. But from that period what partiality! how is the one exalted and the other depressed, by the contrary modes of education which are adopted! the one is taught to aspire, and the other is early confined and limited. As their years increase, the sister must be wholly domesticated, while the brother is led by the hand through all the flowery paths of science. Grant that their minds are by nature equal, yet who shall wonder at the apparent superiority, if indeed custom becomes second nature; nay if it taketh place of nature, and that it doth the experience of each day will evince.

She continues with an argument in favor of full education for girls, though she does not reject the practical division of labor in eighteenth-century society based on gender:

> Will it be urged that those acquirements would supersede our domestick duties. I answer that every requisite in female

economy is easily attained; and, with truth I can add, that when once attained, they require no further mental attention. Nay, while we are pursuing the needle, or the superintendency of the family, I repeat, that our minds are at full liberty for reflection; that imagination may exert itself in full vigour; and that if a just foundation is early laid, our ideas will then be worthy of rational beings. If we were industrious we might easily find time to arrange them upon paper, or should avocations press too hard for such an indulgence, the hours allotted for conversation would at least become more refined and rational. Should it still be vociferated, "Your domestick employments are sufficient"—I would calmly ask, is it reasonable, that a candidate for immortality, for the joys of heaven, an intelligent being, who is to spend an eternity in contemplating the works of Deity, should at present be so degraded, as to be allowed no other ideas, than those which are suggested by the mechanism of a pudding, or the sewing [of] the seams of a garment? Pity that all such censurers of female improvement do not go one step further, and deny their future existence; to be consistent they surely ought.

Yes, ye lordly, ye haughty sex, our souls are by nature equal to yours; the same breath of God animates, enlivens, and invigorates us.

Discussion: Murray argues that women's souls are equal to those of men, and from that argument proceeds her call for developing the minds of women as well as men through equal access to education. Does Murray's eighteenth-century call for women's equality and for equal access to education call us to action in our contemporary world? In what ways?

Connecting with Our Lives

In Our Faith Communities
Judith Sargent Murray makes a theological argument for women's access to education and women's right to express themselves publicly. She held that the souls of women and the souls of men were equally valuable in God's eyes. Invite your small group, youth group, or Coming of Age group to consider what theological or religious arguments Unitarian Universalists in today's world make for the worth of all people.

Organize an event at your church featuring a panel with women of different generations and varied perspectives on feminism and women's rights/equality. Alternatively, interview women of different generations and perspectives, and compile a collection of their reflections on the role feminism has played in their lives.

At Home
Systematic injustice still affects women in today's world. Become involved with an advocacy organization or initiative addressing women's issues in your community or explore the Unitarian Universalist Service Committee's website (www.uusc.org) to find out about some of their partner organizations, particularly those that focus on education, violence prevention, and economic opportunity for women.

Judith Sargent Murray's brothers received an education that was denied to her because she was female. Explore your own family stories about gender expectations and opportunities. To what extent did gender expectations impact the life of your mother, your grandmother, and your great-grandmother (or those of their generations)? To what extent do people today still make decisions about what people should or should not do based on gender?

Find Out More

Cassara, Ernest. "Hosea Ballou." *Dictionary of Unitarian and Universalist Biography*, published online by the Unitarian Universalist Historical Society at www25.uua.org/uuhs.

———, ed. *Universalism in America: A Documentary History*. Boston: Beacon Press, 1971.

Dykeman, Therese Boos. *American Women Philosophers, 1650–1930: Six Exemplary Thinkers*. Lewiston, NY: Edwin Mellen Press, 1993.

Hill, Andrew. "James Relly." *Dictionary of Unitarian and Universalist Biography*, published online by the Unitarian Universalist Historical Society at www25.uua.org/uuhs.

Hughes, Peter. "Caleb Rich." *Dictionary of Unitarian and Universalist Biography*, published online by the Unitarian Universalist Historical Society at www25.uua.org/uuhs.

Murray, John. *The Life of Rev. John Murray, Preacher of Universal Salvation, Written by Himself, with a Continuation, by Mrs. Judith Sargent Murray*. Boston: Universalist Publishing House, 1869. It can be read online at Google Books.

Murray, Judith Sargent Stevens. *Some Deductions from the System Promulgated in the Page of Divine Revelation: Ranged in the Order and Form of a Catechism: Intended as an Assistant to the Christian Parent or Teacher*. Portsmouth, NH and Norwich, CT: John Trumbull, 1782. Republished by Bonnie Hurd Smith as *A Universalist Catechism*, Salem, MA: Hurd Smith Communications, 2009.

Skemp, Sheila L. *First Lady of Letters: Judith Sargent Murray and the Struggle for Female Independence*. Philadelphia: University of Pennsylvania Press, 2009.

———. *Judith Sargent Murray: A Brief Biography with Documents*. Boston: Bedford Books, 1998.

Smith, Bonnie Hurd. "Judith Sargent Murray." *Dictionary of Unitarian and Universalist Biography*, published online by the Unitarian Universalist Historical Society at www25.uua.org/uuhs.

New Ideas about Education

Bronson Alcott and Elizabeth Palmer Peabody's Educational Reform

Amos Bronson Alcott (1799–1888) and Elizabeth Palmer Peabody (1804–1894) believed that the education of young children was a sacred undertaking, concerned with hearts and souls as much as minds. While she was still a teenager, Peabody discussed with William Ellery Channing her idea that "the development of character is the first thing to be aimed at in education, and the communication of knowledge the second." As teacher to Channing's daughter Mary for seven years, Peabody had many opportunities to discuss education with him, and their discussions led them both to a philosophy of education focused on strengthening the child's power of thought and moral discernment, rather than conveying established rules and ways of thinking.

Alcott, who grew up on a farm in Connecticut, developed his own mystical faith in the intuitive insight of children quite independently of Channing's influence. He was a self-taught genius whose only schooling had served to show him how not to teach. As his famous daughter Louisa described his style of teaching, he "taught in the wise way which unfolds what lies in the child's nature, as a flower blooms, rather than crammed it, like a Strasburg goose, with more than it could digest."

Alcott and Peabody, who became members of New England Transcendentalism's inner circle, disapproved of the traditional drill-and-recitation style of teaching and wanted to usher in a new era of education for young children. For a short period in the 1830s, they taught together in one of history's best-known experimental schools: Boston's Temple

School. In 1835, Peabody published her book Record of a School, *which laid out Alcott's philosophy of education and described his interactions with pupils during the Temple School's first year. This story tells about the school—and about how new views of human nature resulted in new ideas about teaching.*

At nine o'clock on a cold January morning in 1835, Miss Elizabeth Peabody climbed to the second floor of the Masonic Temple in Boston. As she reached the spacious schoolroom upstairs, she gazed about approvingly. Sunlight pouring in through a large Gothic window fell on bookcases filled with fine books, and on statues and other works of art that gave the room a quiet dignity. Boys and girls were sitting at their desks, writing diligently in their journals. Their teacher, Mr. Alcott, was walking around the room, preparing pencils and pens at each seat. From time to time, he made remarks to individual children in a soft voice. Two children arrived late and spoke as they entered the classroom. Mr. Alcott sent them back out, to come in quietly.

This scene may appear quaint and old-fashioned, viewed from the twenty-first century, but it describes a school that was radical and revolutionary at the time. The Temple School had an enrollment of about thirty children, who were mostly under the age of ten. This was Bronson Alcott's school, but assisting him was Elizabeth Palmer Peabody, a gifted teacher who taught Latin and a bit of geometry. Her main role was to observe and record what took place. The two of them hoped that this small school would become a model for reforming American education.

In the Temple School, children sat in comfortable chairs at their own desks, which were arranged to face the wall so that they could focus on their work without distraction. When Mr. Alcott was leading a discussion, they turned their chairs around and sat in a semicircle around him. Alcott's model of the ideal teacher was the biblical Jesus, who taught by telling stories and engaging in conversation. Alcott's own teaching method consisted mainly in asking questions and letting children express their thoughts as he guided them to conclusions. He read aloud to them, stopping often to let them consider and comment on what they were learning. He even involved them in discussing and agreeing to the school's rules and punishments.

This was not at all the way most teachers taught. An authoritarian, rote-learning method was standard practice in those days. Children generally sat in straight rows, with furniture that gave no thought to comfort or beauty. They memorized lessons and recited them. The routine was boring and led to much misbehavior. Teachers made ample use of both humiliation and physical punishment to shame or frighten the children into learning. A belief that all children were inherently bad was common at the time, and teachers thought they needed to cudgel and cajole their pupils into giving up their sinful ways.

Bronson Alcott and Elizabeth Peabody held an entirely different view of human nature. They agreed with the poet William Wordsworth, who wrote,

> Trailing clouds of glory do we come
> from God, who is our home:
> Heaven lies about us in our infancy!

Children were not only born innocent; they were closer to God than adults, and thus better able to tap into the divinity of their own nature. Alcott believed that a child's intuition was a path to divine truth. His purpose in teaching was to draw out from children the best of what already lay within them.

At Alcott's school, Elizabeth Peabody wrote down as much as she could of what the children said and did. She was eager to share with the world the wonderful success of Alcott's method. The pupils at the school were unusually attentive throughout the school day, and in the teacher-led conversations, they revealed remarkable insights. Peabody used the notes she had written to create a book called *Record of a School*.

The book made quite a stir. Many people from home and abroad had already come to visit the school, but there was even more interest after the book was published. Alcott became famous. He was so pleased by the success of Peabody's book that he decided to follow it with one of his own. His book focused on a series of conversations about the life and teachings of Jesus. He called the book *Conversations with Children on the Gospels*.

By this time, Peabody had begun to disagree with him on certain points. She also needed to devote more of her time to other work, because Alcott had never been able to pay her. As Alcott prepared *Conversations with Children on the Gospels* for publication, Peabody distanced herself more and more from his work. She was particularly worried about a conversation he wanted to publish that she thought would cause a scandal. The conversation began with the Gospel account of the conception of Jesus and continued on the subject of love and babies. It hinted at a vague sort of sex education, and she urged Alcott to remove it from the book. He decided to keep it in.

As it turned out, Peabody's instincts were right. The first book had made Alcott's school famous, but the second book made it infamous. Controversies raised by the book caused many parents to withdraw their children from Alcott's school. As the school limped along, Alcott, who believed in racial equality, admitted a child of color to the school. This caused another uproar, and the school shut down completely. Alcott's evident success with children could not save him. His reputation was in shambles, and his career as a schoolteacher ended in 1839.

Despite the collapse of the Temple School, Bronson Alcott and Elizabeth Peabody, who were both core members of the group that came to be known as the Transcendentalists, continued separately to advocate for their child-centered educational philosophy. Many of their radical ideas gradually came into the mainstream. Alcott communicated his philosophy to adults through conversations and lectures over the next fifty years. Peabody continued to work for educational reform and eventually founded the first American kindergartens. But the most enduring link between New England Transcendentalism and schools of today may be an indirect one forged by Bronson Alcott's famous daughter.

Louisa May Alcott wrote children's books that were extremely popular and widely read. She created fictional adults who shared her father's educational philosophy. *Little Men,* a book written in 1871, takes place entirely in a school modeled on his ideals. "My father's school was the only one I ever went to," she later wrote, "and when this was broken up because he introduced methods now all the fashion, our lessons went on at home, for he was always sure of four little pupils who firmly believed in their teacher." Louisa's loving portrayal of her father's teaching style undoubtedly impressed more than a few of her young readers, some of whom became teachers themselves. For many generations, ideas and attitudes inspired by Bronson Alcott and Elizabeth Peabody have remained at the heart of progressive education, and they continue to influence teachers today.

Quotations for Discussion

In his journal for September 21, 1828, Bronson Alcott wrote,

> The province of the instructor should be simple, awakening, invigorating, directing, rather than the forcing of the child's faculties upon prescribed and exclusive courses of thought. He should look to the child to see what is to be done, rather than to his book or his system. The Child is the Book. The operations of his mind are the true system. Let him study these carefully and his success is sure. Let him follow out the impulses, the thoughts, the volitions, of the child's mind and heart, in their own principles and rational order of expression, and his training will be what God designed it to be—an aid to prepare the child to aid himself.

Alcott spoke of the primary purpose of education in *The Doctrine and Discipline of Human Culture* (1836). Two excerpts are included here:

Human culture [i.e. Education] is the art of revealing to a man the true Idea of his Being.... It includes all those influences, and disciplines, by which his faculties are unfolded and perfected. It is that agency which takes the helpless and pleading Infant from the hands of its Creator; and, apprehending its entire nature, tempts it forth—now by austere, and now by kindly influences and disciplines—and this moulds it at last into the Image of a Perfect Man.... It seeks to realize in the Soul the Image of the Creator.—Its end is a perfect man.

Yet, dimmed as is the Divine Image in Man, it reflects not the full and fair Image of the Godhead. We seek it alone in Jesus in its fullness; yet sigh to behold it with our corporeal senses. And this privilege God ever vouchsafes to the pure and undefiled heart; for he ever sends it upon the earth in the form of the Child. Herein have we a Type of the Divinity. Herein is our Nature yet despoiled of none of its glory.

Discussion: Alcott's educational philosophy placed an emphasis on drawing out the best of what is already within the child, believing that a teacher who truly understands the impulses, thoughts, and volitions of a child's mind and heart will be able to bring out a "Type of Divinity.... despoiled of none of its glory." How does education serve as a kind of unfolding and perfecting of a person's inner nature?

"To contemplate Spirit in ourselves and in our fellow men, is obviously the only means of understanding social duty, and quickening within ourselves a wise Humanity," writes Elizabeth Palmer Peabody in her preface to the second edition of *Record of a School* (1836). In the Temple School, where most of the pupils were between the ages of six and ten, Mr. Alcott's first priority was not to "make children investigate External nature," but to lead them to a "contemplation of Spirit as it unveils itself within themselves." Peabody further explains,

> No subject interests children so much as self-analysis. To give name to inward movements of heart and mind, whether in themselves or others, is an employment of their faculties which will enchain the attention of the most volatile. There is no one class of objects in external nature, which interests all children; for children are very differently gifted with respect to their sympathies with nature. But all are conscious of something within themselves which moves, thinks, and feels; and as a mere subject of curiosity and investigation, for the sake of knowledge, it may take place of all others. In order to investigate it, a great many things must be done, which are in themselves very agreeable. Mr. Alcott reads, and tells stories, calculated to excite various moral emotions. On these stories, he asks questions, in order to bring out from each, in words, the feelings which have been called forth. These feelings receive their name, and history, and place in the moral scale. Then books, and passages from books are read, calculated to exercise various intellectual faculties, such as Perception, Imagination, Judgment, Reason (both in apprehension and comprehension); and these various exercises of mind are discriminated and named. . . . There is not a single thing that cannot be studied with comparative ease, by a child, who can be taught what faculties he must use, and how they are to be brought to bear on the subject, and what influence on those faculties the subject will have, after it is mastered.

Discussion: Alcott and Peabody argue for education that emphasizes a kind of metacognition—a knowing about knowing. They believed in helping children understand themselves through naming and understanding the emotions they feel and the different modes of thinking they use. The Temple School focused on helping children learn how to learn. To what extent does contemporary educational practice reflect this point of view? To what extent is it in conflict with Alcott and Peabody's point of view? How does today's Unitarian Universalist religious education and faith development reflect this point of view?

◎

The following is an excerpt of a conversation on the subject of obedience from *Record of a School*:

> Some of the little ones said, we must obey the Ten Commandments; fathers and mothers; the Lord; and one said, our Own Spirit. How do you find out, said Mr. Alcott to him, when you want to know what is right and what is wrong? I ask Conscience. Another boy said, I ask my parents. A case was stated in which the parents could not be near? and it was asked, how should you do then? I don't know. Would not conscience tell you? If I knew which was right, conscience would tell me to do it. You must know first, then, before conscience would speak? Yes. (This boy was seven years old.)
>
> Another boy then asked, if one's parents should tell me to kill somebody, would it be right to do it? What do you think? said Mr. Alcott. I think it would not be right, said he. Why? Because God commands us not to do wrong. You would know it was wrong then, even if your parents did not tell you so? Yes.

On another day, after an interesting conversation about the relationship of soul to body, Mr. Alcott continued,

> Now go forth into the external world and find some fact or appearance, in the external world, with which to picture out and typify birth. They were quite animated by this and the following were the most striking analogies. One said,

the seed sown, and springing up. What do you mean by the seed, body or soul? Both. Another said, the branches from the trunk. The soul is the trunk, and the branches the body. Another said, I should think the trunk was God, and the branches were the soul. Another said, the soul is a rose-bud putting forth leaves. Another said, God is a rock, and we are pieces broken off. Violently? No, not violently. The next said, God is the water, and our souls are drops; he afterwards added, that God was the only real person, and we were pictures of him. God is the ocean, and we are the rivers, said the next. Another said, God is a sower, and we are the seeds which he sows. Mr. Alcott said, I have had that image myself; listen to these lines: [He read nine lines of verse, not included here.]

Another boy said, the seed is God, and we are the fruit that springs out of it. Another said, God is the earth, and we are the productions. Another said, God is the shepherd, and we are the sheep. Mr. Alcott said, that is Scripture phraseology; but Jesus is generally called the shepherd. One of the little girls said, God is the Sun, and Jesus Christ is the Moon, and we are the stars. You mean, said Mr. Alcott, that Jesus is superior to us, and God is superior to all, and gives his light to Jesus? Yes. That is the best one of all, said the rest. . . .

Mr. Alcott allowed these analogies to run on, that they all might clearly understand the principle of metaphor. At last he said, these are analogies, and many of them are good, but none are perfect; for there is nothing in the vegetable or animal world, which is quite adequate to typify the great fact of birth, the incarnation, or embodying of the spirit.

Discussion: How did children learn from Alcott's encouragement of their questions and responses? Have you ever had a conversation with a child about some of the mysteries of life? What did you learn from the conversation? What do you think the child/children learned?

Connecting with Our Lives

In Our Faith Communities
Invite participants in small groups or covenant groups to consider Bronson Alcott's and Elizabeth Peabody's belief that children are born pure and good. Ask them to think about whether wicked actions and moral weaknesses are the result of a person's inborn nature or of a person's upbringing. Calvinists came down on the side of nature, believing that infants were born sinners. Followers of John Locke came down on the side of upbringing, believing that children were born as "blank slates" and developed according to the influences in their environment. Encourage the group to discuss where their individual beliefs fall along the nature versus nurture continuum. Invite further reflection on whether every child has a capacity for evil as well as for good and to what extent environmental influences determine the way our inborn capacities develop. Ask them to consider to what extent each of us has a moral compass—a conscience that distinguishes right from wrong, no matter what happens to us or what the people around us do and say.

To investigate how education changes over time, talk to teachers who learned to teach in different eras about methods of teaching and attitudes toward children's learning. You might organize a conversation among people of different generations in your faith community about their school experience and how it has influenced them.

At Home
The Transcendentalists believed in the perfectibility of individuals and of society. They believed that education was of utmost importance. Discuss the importance of education in your family. What is education for? Is it to learn how to support yourself and accomplish life tasks? Is it to become a better member of society? Is it a matter of personal satisfaction—learning what you truly want to know? Make sure that people of all ages are included in your family conversation.

Bronson Alcott broke with convention in many ways, some of which offended people, most notably when he allowed young children to discuss conception and birth, even if only in metaphorical ways, and when he admitted a child of color to his school. Find examples of ways in which contemporary educators break with convention and find themselves at the center of controversy. What are the educational issues that cause controversy in your local area? How have you responded to controversy surrounding the philosophy, methodology, and content of education in your local school system? Find ways to advocate for your point of view.

Find Out More

Alcott, A. Bronson. *The Doctrine and Discipline of Human Culture.* Boston: James Monroe and Company, 1836. It can be read online at Google Books.

Alcott, Louisa May. *Little Men: Life at Plumfield with Jo's Boys.* Originally published 1871. Many editions are available.

———. "Recollections of My Childhood," reprinted in *Louisa May Alcott: An Intimate Anthology.* New York: Doubleday, 1997.

Buell, Lawrence. *The American Transcendentalists: Essential Writings.* New York: Modern Library, 2006.

Goodwin, Joan. "Louisa May Alcott." *Dictionary of Unitarian and Universalist Biography*, published online by the Unitarian Universalist Historical Society at www25.uua.org/uuhs.

Howe, Charles, and Peter Hughes. "Bronson and Abigail Alcott." *Dictionary of Unitarian and Universalist Biography*, published online by the Unitarian Universalist Historical Society at www25.uua.org/uuhs.

Marshall, Megan. *The Peabody Sisters: Three Women Who Ignited American Romanticism.* Boston: Houghton Mifflin, 2005.

Matteson, John. *Eden's Outcasts: The Story of Louisa May Alcott and Her Father.* New York: W. W. Norton, 2007.

Peabody, Elizabeth Palmer. *Record of a School: Exemplifying the General Principles of Spiritual Culture.* 2nd ed. Boston: Russell, Shattuck, 1836. It can be read online at Google Books.

———. *Record of Mr. Alcott's School: Exemplifying the Principles and Methods of Moral Culture.* 3rd ed., rev. Boston: Roberts Brothers, 1874. It can be read online at Google Books.

Ritchie, Susan. "Elizabeth Palmer Peabody." *Dictionary of Unitarian and Universalist Biography*, published online by the Unitarian Universalist Historical Society at www25.uua.org/uuhs.

Shepard, Odell. *Pedlar's Progress: The Life of Bronson Alcott.* Boston: Little, Brown, 1937.

Margaret Fuller's New View of Womanhood

Margaret Fuller (1810–1850) taught at Bronson Alcott's Temple School from December 1836 until April 1837. Although Fuller already had a famous knack for engaging people in conversation, the chance to observe Alcott's discussion method gave her new ideas about using the art of conversation in teaching. As a conversationalist, Margaret Fuller far surpassed even Alcott. Judging from the many accounts left by people who knew her, it would seem that she had no peer. Her personal magnetism was legendary.

Sadly, we can never experience the special power of Margaret Fuller's conversations. We can know her only from her writing and from what people have said about her, and these are very imperfect records. Much of her writing seems ponderous today, filled with references and allusions that are obscure to the twenty-first century reader. Meanwhile, the written accounts left by people who knew her are wildly contradictory and paint a confusing portrait. As her dear friend James Freeman Clarke wrote, "Margaret had so many aspects to her soul that she might furnish material for a hundred biographers, not all could be said even then."

Nonetheless, we do know many important things about Margaret Fuller. We know that she wrote about women's rights in a way that inspired others to action. We know that she was the first editor of the Dial, *the most important philosophical and literary journal of the Transcendentalists. We know that she was the first woman to be hired as a literary critic for a major U.S. newspaper (Horace Greeley's* New York Tribune*), and that she was also that paper's first foreign correspondent. We know that she was an active participant in the Italian revolution of*

1848 and that she died at age forty in a shipwreck, as she was returning to America with her Italian husband and their small son. Margaret Fuller's personality was powerful, and she affected the people of her day in ways that have had a lasting influence. This story focuses on her role in helping to unleash women's intellectual capabilities and redefine women's place in society.

What did it mean to be a woman in the nineteenth century? This was the central question of Margaret Fuller's life. Unlike most girls of her time, she had not been brought up to believe that her mind was inferior. Her father had educated her as if she were a boy bound for college. By her early teens, Margaret was an impressive young scholar—and she expressed her ideas with unusual clarity and confidence.

Unfortunately, these were not qualities that made a girl popular in the 1820s—not even in the highbrow community of Cambridge, Massachusetts, where she lived. As Margaret entered society, her parents suddenly realized that her education had failed to foster the social graces that a woman required. To remedy the situation, they packed her off to Miss Susan Prescott's Young Ladies' Seminary, a boarding school in the remote town of Groton, Massachusetts. Margaret protested that she would have to give up her studies of Latin, Italian, and Greek—the subjects that interested her most. But to her parents, the development of a "modest & unassuming deportment" now seemed far more important than Greek.

After a year at Miss Prescott's, Margaret returned home, determined to continue her classical education. She studied doggedly, preferring not to face the question of "What next?" College was not an option, of course; no colleges admitted women. But she was fortunate to live near Harvard, and she formed a number of lasting friendships with students there who accepted her as their intellectual equal. She became known as a superb conversationalist and was surrounded by a circle of friends, both male and female.

Not until she was in her early twenties did Margaret fully face the reality of her situation as a woman. Her father purchased a farm in 1833 and moved the entire family to rural Groton. Margaret felt isolated and despondent. Her male friends were beginning their careers, and her female friends were getting married. She was beginning to fear that her own life was leading nowhere.

Given her limited options, Margaret decided to become a writer. She began thinking about an ambitious project: the biography of a German author she greatly admired. When an older couple she had known in Cambridge invited her to travel to Europe with them, Margaret was eager to go—and not just for enjoyment. She wanted to gather information for her writing. Margaret's parents consented to the trip even though they had been counting on her to educate her four youngest siblings. Departure was planned for the summer of 1836. She was to be away for a year and a half.

Then the unthinkable happened. Margaret's father died suddenly, leaving no will. His estate was difficult to settle, and Margaret and her mother were denied control of it because they were women. The Fullers found themselves impoverished and at the mercy of one of Margaret's uncles, whose management of affairs made their lives miserable. The burden of keeping the family together and finding means for their support fell largely to twenty-five-year-old Margaret Fuller. She gave up all hope of traveling to Europe.

Some of her friends suggested to Ralph Waldo Emerson and his wife that an invitation to visit Concord might help lift Margaret's spirits. The Emersons obliged, and she stayed with them for three weeks in the summer of 1836. It marked the beginning of a very important friendship.

Emerson's first impression of Margaret Fuller was not favorable, but she quickly won him over. As he later noted, it was common for men who knew her only by reputation to view her with suspicion and even dislike. Yet those who actually met her were surprised to discover how much they liked her. According to Emerson, "The ease with which she entered into conversation made them forget all they had heard of her." They soon found themselves confiding in her. Fuller had a rare gift for bringing out the best in her companions, and people she conversed with often remarked that she had opened doors to a new way of thinking.

As it turned out, the Concord visit opened doors for Fuller too. One door opened when Emerson's friend Bronson Alcott stopped by. Elizabeth Peabody, his teaching assistant at the Temple School in Boston, was leaving the school. Alcott offered the position to Fuller. She agreed to join him in Boston as soon as she had helped her mother prepare for the winter in Groton. In December 1836, she settled in at the Temple School, teaching languages in the morning and recording Alcott's conversations in the afternoon. In the evenings, she taught college-level literature courses to young women.

By April, Alcott could no longer afford to keep Fuller on at the school. She accepted a teaching position at a school in Providence, Rhode Island, founded by one of Alcott's admirers. She used conversations in her teaching there with great success. The older girls at the school adored her. But Fuller was not happy in Providence. The cultural life there was no match for Boston, and her health was poor. Teaching left her no energy for writing.

She returned to Massachusetts and launched a new venture in the fall of 1839: a series of conversations for "well-educated and thinking women." Fuller had observed that girls learned many subjects in school, but they were rarely asked to apply what they learned. She planned to use the discussion method to help women bring clarity and precision to their thinking. Women were invited to enroll in a series of weekly Conversations, one series beginning in November, another in March. Each series would explore a particular topic, such as Greek mythology or the fine arts, but the primary purpose was for women to consider the "great questions"—"What were we born to do? How shall we do it?"

The Conversations were enormously successful and continued for four years. Twenty-five women joined the first series, and after that, each series had more than thirty subscribers. Many were the wives, daughters, and sisters of prominent men. Some were authors, reformers, or teachers in their own right. After the last series in 1844, Fuller published a book called *Woman in the Nineteenth Century* that brought the ideas she had explored in the Conversations to a much wider audience.

Margaret Fuller challenged the fundamental assumptions that governed the roles of women and men in society. She argued that the female side of human nature is in no way inferior to the male, and that society could approach perfection only when women and men respected each other equally and had equal opportunities to flourish. In the nineteenth century, men held such disproportionate influence that women had little sense of what they could achieve. "I believe that, at present, women are the best helpers of one another," Fuller wrote. "Let them think; let them act; till they know what they need."

By this insight, and by the example of her own life, Margaret Fuller inspired women to work together in the pursuit of wider goals. Women's clubs and colleges sprang up in her wake. Changes in laws concerning marriage and property became a reality. A new sense of female solidarity grew as women worked together in pursuit of "self-culture," education, and reform. By questioning society's most basic assumptions about gender differences and by encouraging open discussion of these issues, Margaret Fuller nurtured women's self-confidence. She helped them begin to define their own lives.

Quotations for Discussion

"Conversation is my natural element. I need to be called out, and never think alone, without imagining some companion." wrote Margaret Fuller. Although we will never know exactly what Margaret Fuller's weekly two-hour Conversation sessions were like, two participants, Caroline Dall and Elizabeth Peabody, wrote summaries of some of them. From them, we can see how ideas explored in the Conversations were later presented in Fuller's best-known work,

Woman in the Nineteenth Century. The following excerpt from the Conversations, summarized by Elizabeth Peabody, is one example:

> Miss Fuller thought that the man and the woman had each every faculty and element of mind—but they were combined in different proportions. . . .
> Ellen [Hooper] asked if she thought that there was any quality in the masculine or in the feminine mind that did not belong to the other. Margaret said no—she did not.

In *Woman in the Nineteenth Century*, Fuller writes: "Let it not be said, wherever there is energy or creative genius, 'She has a masculine mind.' . . . There is no wholly masculine man, no purely feminine woman."

Discussion: Fuller's Conversations led the women who participated to new understanding by encouraging them to question some of the prevailing assumptions of the time about women and their capacity for creativity and deep thinking. When have you been part of a conversation that led you to a new perspective or understanding about your own position in society, history, or culture?

⑥

Ednah Dow Cheney (1824–1904) attended three complete seasons of Fuller's Conversations. She was one of the youngest members of the group, joining when she was just sixteen. When she published her *Reminiscences* in 1902, Cheney included a lengthy remembrance of Margaret Fuller:

> I was eager enough for any intellectual advantage, but I had imbibed with the unthinking eagerness of a schoolgirl the common prejudices against Miss Fuller, and although I believed that I should learn from her, I had no idea that I should esteem and, much more, love her. I found myself in a new world of thought; a flood of light irradiated all that I had seen in nature, observed in life, or read in books. What-

ever she spoke of revealed a hidden meaning, and everything seemed to be put into true relation. Perhaps I could best express it by saying that I was no longer the limitation of myself, but I felt that the whole wealth of the universe was open to me....

One day when she was alone with me, and I feel as if I could now feel her touch and hear her voice, she said, "Is life rich to you?" and I replied, "It is since I have known you." Such was the response of many a youthful heart to her, and herein was her wonderful influence. She did not make us her disciples, her blind followers. She opened the book of life to us and helped us to read it for ourselves....

The first mistake that the world has made in its effort to comprehend this large nature is in considering her, not as a typical woman, but as an exceptional one, whose powers were masculine, and who wielded some magic sword which she alone had strength to grasp.... With all the force of her intellect, all the strength of her will, all her self-denial and power of thought, she was essentially and thoroughly a woman, and she won her victories not by borrowing the peculiar weapons of man, but by using her own with courage and skill.

Another young woman who began attending Margaret Fuller's conversations in her late teens was Caroline Wells Healy Dall (1822–1912). In her 1895 essay, "Transcendentalism as Feminist Heresy," she writes,

> It is hopeless to convey to those who never saw her any idea of Margaret Fuller, to give to those who never lived in the circle that she inspired any impression of her being and influence. She was not beautiful, people said; but she was more than beautiful. A sort of glow surrounded her, and warmed those who listened.... I consider it the greatest blessing of my life that I was admitted almost as a child to the circle that surrounded her, and felt from my first conscious moments the noble atmosphere that she diffused. Among the girls of that

circle one saw no low, ignoble motives, no vanity, no poor ambitions, no coquetries, no looking to marriage as an end, no proneness to idle gossip. Margaret's life began in the constant sacrifice of personal aims to the material wants of her family. It continued, . . . attracting larger and larger crowds of women as long as she had strength to speak, until men who knew her begged admittance to her audience. This granted, she was no longer her best self. It was only with women that she became both priestess and oracle. . . . I do not think I am mistaken in saying that what is meant by New England Transcendentalism perished with Margaret Fuller.

Discussion: Acting as a mentor for the young women in her circle, Fuller helped them gain confidence in their own strengths. Have you had similar experiences with mentors who were able to draw you out and help you to grow in understanding? Which of Fuller's personal qualities as a mentor are echoed in your experiences with your own mentors?

Margaret Fuller became a frequent guest at the Emerson home in Concord, Massachusetts. In *Memoirs of Margaret Fuller Ossoli*, put together by Ralph Waldo Emerson, William Henry Channing, and James Freeman Clarke after her death, Emerson wrote this about her visits,

> Her arrival was a holiday. . . . All tasks that could be suspended were put aside to catch the favourable hour, in walking, riding, or boating, to talk with this joyful guest, who brought wit, anecdotes, love-stories, tragedies, oracles with her, and with her broad web of relations to so many fine friends, seemed like the queen of some parliament of love, who carried the key to all confidences. . . . She drew her companions to surprising confessions. She was the wedding-guest, to whom the long-pent story must be told. . . .

[Her conversations] interested me in every manner—talent, memory, wit, stern introspection, poetic play, religion, the finest personal feeling, the aspects of the future, each followed each in full activity, and left me, I remember, enriched and sometimes astonished by the gifts of my guest.

Discussion: What images, emotions, and thoughts come to mind as you read Emerson's words? What picture of Fuller do they paint? Have you ever been in her position as the center of a social circle, or been acquainted with someone who played a similar role?

Although Margaret Fuller seems never to have known about Judith Sargent Murray's essays, which had argued decades earlier for equality of educational opportunity, *Woman in the Nineteenth Century* makes many of the same points and articulates a case for equality that rests on a religious worldview similar to Murray's. At the soul level, Fuller maintains, women and men are equal—both come from the same "common home" in God. But her vision of a woman's nature "growing" and "unfolding" is typical of New England Transcendentalism and different from the rationalistic eighteenth-century perspective of Judith Sargent Murray:

> We would have every arbitrary barrier thrown down. We would have every path laid open to Woman as freely as to Man. Were this done, and a slight temporary fermentation allowed to subside, we should see crystallizations more pure and of more various beauty. We believe the divine energy would pervade nature to a degree unknown in the history of former ages, and that no discordant collision, but a ravishing harmony of the spheres, would ensue.
>
> Yet, then and only then will mankind be ripe for this, when inward and outward freedom for Woman as much as for Man shall be acknowledged as a right, not yielded as a concession. As the friend of the negro assumes that one

man cannot by right hold another in bondage, so should the friend of Woman assume that Man cannot by right lay even well-meant restrictions on Woman. If the negro be a soul, if the woman be a soul, apparelled in flesh, to one Master only are they accountable. There is but one law for souls, and, if there is to be an interpreter of it, he must come not as man, or son of man, but as son of God. . . . What Woman needs is not as a woman to act or rule, but as a nature to grow, as an intellect to discern, as a soul to live freely and unimpeded, to unfold such powers as were given her when we left our common home.

Discussion: On what philosophical or theological basis do Fuller's arguments for equality rest? How are her arguments similar to or different from the ones contemporary Unitarian Universalists might make in advocating for gender equality?

Connecting with Our Lives

In Our Faith Communities
Margaret Fuller wanted all doors open. She did not advocate that women behave as men, but that they fulfill their own souls' desires. She did not value masculine traits over feminine, believing as she did that the feminine side brings special qualities to the world that the world needs. She also believed that feminine qualities are not unique to women but are found in varying degrees in men, just as qualities identified by society as masculine exist in many women. "In families that I know," she wrote, "some little girls like to saw wood, others to use carpenters' tools. Where these tastes are indulged, cheerfulness and good-humor are promoted. Where they are forbidden, because 'such things are not proper for girls,' they grow sullen and mischievous."

In your youth group, Coming of Age group, covenant group, or discussion group, consider contemporary gender role expectations in our society. Invite participants to name some activities or personality traits that people today consider "girlish" or "boyish." Discuss the subtle, or not so subtle, price people pay when they blur or cross the socially prescribed lines between genders in dress, activities, or other gender expressions. Ask the group to reflect on what their reactions and responses to this question say about the relative status of men and women and about the ways in which society enforces gender norms.

Bronson Alcott often led children in conversations based on the meanings of words themselves—delving into literal and figurative meanings, as well as mental associations of such words as *mind, love, spirit, sign, rich, bliss*. Margaret Fuller adopted this technique and based sessions of the Conversations on topics such as beauty and life.

Offer a series of Fuller-style facilitated conversations on words such as *feminine, masculine, intelligence, intuition, creativity,* and *success*, inviting youth and adults of all ages and life stages to participate. Encourage conversation participants to delve deeply and broadly into participants' feelings about and experiences with these words.

At Home

Margaret Fuller was committed above all to self-improvement. She had tremendous demands on her time from family obligations, household drudgery, friends she wanted to keep in touch with, and the need to earn money. She also suffered from frequent and very painful migraine headaches. But she didn't let duties and frailties keep her from actively pursuing her interests. There were things she wanted to learn, projects she wanted to complete, and people she wanted to meet. Her goals helped her soar above the mundane occupations of everyday life.

Today we are free of many of the demanding household chores that filled so much of a nineteenth-century woman's life. Yet on the whole, we seem no more likely to pursue our loftiest dreams than people were in Fuller's day. Setting self-improvement goals can become a personal or family ritual that you do each year. Write down one or more goals to pursue in the coming year, including a major lifetime goal if there is something you hope to achieve some day. Write down some steps you could take in the coming year toward reaching your goals. Then put the written pages away in a safe place. Choose a time for reflection every year, such as New Year's Eve, or the beginning of the school year. Revisit your goals, record the steps you have taken to reach them, and write down new steps to take or goals to achieve in the coming year. Have a conversation with friends or family members about your hopes and aspirations, your pride in your accomplishments, and your frustrations when goals have not been met. Think of ways to support each other in meeting personal goals.

Find Out More

Andrews, Barry, ed. *The Spirit Leads: Margaret Fuller in Her Own Words*. Boston: Skinner House, 2010.

Buell, Lawrence. *The American Transcendentalists: Essential Writings*. New York: Modern Library, 2006.

Capper, Charles. *Margaret Fuller: An American Romantic Life, Vol. 1: The Private Years*. New York: Oxford University Press, 1992.

Goodwin, Joan. "Margaret Fuller." *Dictionary of Unitarian and Universalist Biography*, published online by the Unitarian Universalist Historical Society at www25.uua.org/uuhs.

Meyerson, Joel, ed. *Fuller in Her Own Time: A Biographical Chronicle of Her Life Drawn from Recollections, Interviews, and Memoirs by Family, Friends, and Associates*. Iowa City: University of Iowa Press, 2008.

Ossoli, Margaret Fuller. *Woman in the Nineteenth Century and Kindred Papers Relating to the Sphere, Condition, and Duties, of Woman*. ed. Arthur B. Fuller. Boston: John. P. Jewett and Company; 1855. It can be read online at Google Books.

Von Mehren, Joan. *Minerva and the Muse: A Life of Margaret Fuller*. Amherst: University of Massachusetts Press, 1994.

Making the Ideal Real at Brook Farm

In 1840, Elizabeth Palmer Peabody established the Foreign Library with a bookshop at 13 West Street in Boston. It became the locus for much Transcendentalist activity. Margaret Fuller's Conversations were held there, the Dial *was published there, and plans were made there for an experiment in communal living that became known as Brook Farm. The official name of the famous community in its early years was The Brook Farm Institute of Agriculture and Education. As Elizabeth Peabody wrote in her article "Plan of the West Roxbury Community," published in the* Dial *in 1842, the community embodied the Transcendentalist yearning to "be rich, not in the metallic representative of wealth, but in the wealth itself, which money should represent; namely, LEISURE TO LIVE IN ALL THE FACULTIES OF THE SOUL" (the capital letters are hers).*

The Brook Farm community was the brainchild of Unitarian Transcendentalist thinkers George Ripley (1802–1880) and his wife, Sophia Willard Dana Ripley (1803–1861). George Ripley was an outspoken Transcendentalist minister, who often found himself at odds with the Unitarian establishment. He left his Boston church in 1841 to establish Brook Farm. Sophia Ripley had been a regular participant in Margaret Fuller's Conversations and, before her marriage, had run her own school. They were joined by a number of other Unitarians, but the community had no religious requirement, nor was it socialist or communist in the usual sense. It was formed as a joint stock company, with payments of fixed interest to the subscribers, and fully supported individual freedoms within the bounds of a community where each was expected to contribute to the common good. Brook Farm strove to find a balance between physical labor and individual self-culture. In 1843, at its largest, it consisted of about one hundred people.

Unfortunately, the land they chose for the farm was rocky and poor, and only one member of the original community was an experienced farmer. As the community struggled to survive, it had two distinct phases. The first years are generally known as the Transcendental period. The second phase began in January 1844, when Brook Farm's constitution was revised. Hoping to get on a sounder financial footing, the community adopted the organizational ideas of Charles Fourier (1772–1837), a French socialist whose theory of labor freely chosen and shared in carefully designed communities was widely publicized in America. By adopting Fourierism, Brook Farm succeeded in attracting new members from the wider community of Fourierists—but they also lost members who disliked the new philosophy, which structured the community more rigidly. In the end, Fourierism contributed to a decline in school enrollment, which had always been Brook Farm's main source of income.

Brook Farm lasted only a short time, from 1841 to 1847, and most people agree that its early years were its best. But the vast majority of those who lived there, regardless of when, had fond memories. As one Brook Farmer later quipped, "There were never such witty potato patches and sparkling cornfields before or since."

On a Saturday afternoon in early June, a girl named Kate was traveling in a horse-drawn bus from Boston, Massachusetts, to her new home at Brook Farm in West Roxbury, a distance of nine miles. The year was 1843, and she was fifteen years old. "I shall never forget the impression that Brook Farm and its people made upon me," she later wrote. "My mother, my young brother and I found ourselves at the door of the 'Hive,' the principal building of the Farm.... and here our community life began."

After the recent death of Kate's father, her mother had met some members of the Brook Farm association. She liked what she heard about this experimental community founded by Transcendentalist thinkers and decided to join them. For Kate's mother, life at Brook Farm promised relief from the loneliness of being a single parent, as well as a chance to provide an excellent education for her children.

Kate had been dreading this new life, but she soon embraced it. "The surroundings were very beautiful," she wrote. "Upon the afternoon of our arrival the 'Hive' was the scene of activity. A dance was to be given that night and all the girls, several of whom were near my own age, were to wear wreaths of wild daisies.... The girls made a wreath for me and were so cordial and kindly... I remember thinking that it was strange that I felt so much at home already. ... Early on Monday morning, after a quiet, restful Sunday, while the older members were engaged in the necessary duties of the farm and household, school work began for the younger people."

The school, Kate discovered, had some extraordinary teachers and courses in English literature, moral philosophy, mathematics, modern languages, history, Greek, Latin, botany, music, and drawing. They also had a dance instructor and a variety of interesting visitors, including Ralph Waldo Emerson, Margaret Fuller, Elizabeth Peabody, and Bronson Alcott, who provided lectures and conversations.

Every pupil in the school, and every member of the association, was expected to devote from one to four hours a day to manual labor: farming, gardening, care of animals, or some form of housework. They chose their jobs as inclination or natural aptitude suggested. "For this work, we were paid ten cents an hour," Kate explained, "and the amount credited to us was deducted from the regular bills. . . . But our daily life was not given up entirely to study and work. There was an amusement group made up from the instructors and older members, whose business it was to provide entertainment. Dancing parties, picnics, musicals, pageants, plays, rural fetes and tableaux filled up our leisure hours."

A boy who spent a year at Brook Farm later recalled, "I was one of the scholars; and very little did I learn. That was my own fault. I have never regretted my idleness. I was too busy in the fields and by the river to study. . . . We Brook Farmers were exceedingly happy people, and perfectly satisfied with our little isolated circle. ... The life was pure, the company choice. There was a great deal of hard work, and plenty of fun."

A school with extraordinary teachers, where young people went to classes—or not—as they chose, where they worked and played on a farm alongside their teachers in a community of all ages—surely this was one of the most unusual experiments in the history of education. And by all accounts, it was one of the happiest too. How had such a school come to be?

The idea for the Brook Farm school and community was conceived in part as a result of the economic depression of 1837. At that time, a Unitarian minister in Boston named George Ripley saw many people suffering from poverty or beset with anxiety about their finances. "The great danger of our country," he said, "... is the inordinate pursuit, the extravagant worship of wealth." He urged his congregation to "learn from what we are now going through, to cherish a deeper sense of our dependence upon one another." His parishioners had little interest in ideas about reform though. In 1840, Ripley decided he should leave the ministry to begin a life of social action in a different sphere.

Ripley and his wife, Sophia, gradually settled on a plan. They decided to establish a community that would provide a model for how people could live cooperatively. They tried to persuade their Transcendentalist friends to join them. The community would seek to "insure a more natural union between intellectual and manual labor than now exists," George Ripley wrote to his friend Emerson. At his new community, he would "combine the thinker and the worker, as far as possible, in the same individual."

Most members of the Transcendental Club chose not to join, but in April 1841, George and Sophia Ripley, along with a small band of supporters, moved to a farm that they hoped could sustain their community. Education was one of the primary purposes of Brook Farm from the start. "We are a company of teachers," wrote George Ripley. "The branch of industry which we pursue as our primary object and chief means of support is teaching." The Brook

Farmers ran an infant school, a primary school, a college preparatory school, and a three-year course in agriculture. They also had an active program of adult education.

One of the most unusual features of Brook Farm was the equal treatment of men and women. Women were paid the same amount for an hour's work as men and had a voice in the running of the community. As a cofounder of Brook Farm, Sophia Ripley set an example for the full participation of women in whatever areas of labor and leadership they chose.

A popular saying among the Brook Farmers was "idealize the actual." It encouraged people to view things in a positive light— even if only humorously, as when they referred to the manure pile as the Gold Mine. Humor was an important part of daily life at Brook Farm, along with lively conversation and camaraderie. The positive attitude of the leaders seems to have had an uplifting effect on the whole community. Surviving accounts indicate that people really were more thoughtful, more helpful, and more cheerful at Brook Farm than in the world at large. John Sears, a student there, recalled that "sincere and even affectionate cordiality was the distinguishing characteristic of the Brook Farmers in their relations with each other. . . . This was the outward showing of the inward spirit of Brook Farm. It was loving kindness exemplified."

Today, we remember Brook Farm not for idealizing the actual but for trying to actualize the ideal. The entire experiment began as an attempt to turn Transcendentalist idealism into a practical reality. For a brief shining moment in the 1840s, there existed a small community committed to equal rights, harmony, and happiness; a community of individuals who believed in improving their bodies, minds, and hearts through a balance of physical, intellectual, and social activity; a community that honored the arts but equally respected the simple necessity of manual labor.

Unfortunately, Brook Farm began on a shaky financial foundation, which grew ever less stable until the community was forced to disband in 1847. But those who had thrived in its school would never forget the joy of learning in an atmosphere that was free of anxiety and competition. They would never forget that they had once had the privilege of living and working with high-minded women and men who were cheerfully striving to make the ideal real.

Quotations for Discussion

The ideals of Brook Farm are spelled out in the preamble to the Brook Farm Association's 1844 Constitution:

> In order more effectually to promote the great purposes of human culture; to establish the external relations of life on a basis of wisdom and purity; to apply the principles of justice and love to our social organization in accordance with the laws of Divine Providence; to substitute a system of brotherly cooperation for one of selfish competition; to secure to our children and those who may be entrusted to our care the benefits of the highest physical, intellectual, and moral education, which in the progress of knowledge the resources at our command will permit; to institute an attractive, efficient, and productive system of industry; to prevent the exercise of worldly anxiety, by the competent supply of our necessary wants; to diminish the desire of excessive accumulation, by making the acquisition of individual property subservient to upright and disinterested uses; to guarantee to each other forever the means of physical support, and of spiritual progress; and thus to impart a greater freedom, simplicity, truthfulness, refinement, and moral dignity, to our mode of life;—we the undersigned do unite in a voluntary Association, and adopt and ordain the following articles of agreement.

Discussion: Which clauses of the preamble to the Brook Farm constitution speak most clearly to your own vision of an ideal community? What would it be like to be part of such a noble experiment?

George Ripley, along with Frederic Henry Hedge, was a founder of what became known as the Transcendental Club. The first meeting was held at the Ripleys' home in 1836. Some members of the group, like Emerson, emphasized individual self-perfection, while others, like Ripley, came to focus more and more on societal reform. Although the two groups remained loyal friends and supporters, they traveled on different paths. In 1840, George Ripley described his beliefs as follows:

> There is a class of persons who desire a reform in the prevailing philosophy of the day. These are called Transcendentalists,— because they believe in an order of truths which transcends the sphere of the external senses. Their leading idea is the supremacy of mind over matter. Hence they maintain that the truth of religion does not depend on tradition, or on historical facts, but has an unerring witness in the soul. There is a light, they believe, which enlighteneth every man that cometh into the world; there is a faculty in all, the most degraded, the most ignorant, the most obscure, to perceive spiritual truth, when distinctly repented; and the ultimate appeal, on all moral questions is not to a jury of scholars, a hierarchy of divines, or the prescriptions of a creed, but to the common sense of the race. These views I have always adopted; they have been at the foundation of my preaching. . . .
>
> There is another class of persons who are devoted to the removal of the abuses that prevail in modern society. They witness the oppressions done under the sun and they cannot keep silence. They have faith that God governs man; they believe in a better future than the past; their daily prayer is for the coming of the kingdom of righteousness, truth and love; they look forward to a more pure, more lovely, more divine state of society than was ever realized on earth. With these views I rejoice to say I strongly and entirely sympathize.

Discussion: Ripley speaks of two approaches: cultivation of the individual soul and the removal of abuses in society. How are they compatible? Must one choose one approach over another? How do the same differences in expression and practice prevail in your own faith community today?

In aspiring toward a cooperative society, the Brook Farm community did not lose sight of the Transcendentalist commitment to individual self-improvement. In a letter to Ralph Waldo Emerson, Sophia Ripley wrote,

> You can hardly realize, how unimportant the results of our undertaking, or any undertaking seem to me, except that of leading the noblest life. As removing some of the external obstacles to such a life, for myself & others, I chiefly value our scheme, & gratefully accept cooperation; but it is not as cooperators, but as men & women that I look on our friends, & demand no more of them for being here; only hoping that a healthier atmosphere may furnish a better chance for vigorous growth.

Discussion: Have you experienced being part of a community, even if for a short time, that was based on ideals or a vision for how people ought to live? Such groups might include housing cooperatives, affinity groups, faith communities, and conference communities. If you have had such an experience, do you agree that "a healthier atmosphere may furnish a better chance for vigorous growth"?

The following excerpt is from a letter written by a young man at Brook Farm on December 11, 1845. He begins by explaining what it was like to live in an "Association" and ends the letter this way:

Since I came here I find my ideas all changed in relation to this subject. Instead of the yoke that I felt would be on me, I find freedom—freedom to speak, to act, and a truly self-imposed government. The yoke I expected to find is very easy and the burden is light. I enjoy my life and home. We have not much of worldly goods, but we are united and we look high up—some say to cloud-land; but I assure you that on the average there is nowhere a clearer-headed set of persons on social questions than here, and association is now to me the most beautiful thing on earth. The life and ideas are all one with harmony. Surely is it not better for me to begin life this way than with doubt and distrust of my fellows? Doubt begets doubt; faith begets faith; action begets action. If we can get enough persons to follow us, we can prove whether our ideas are true or not. Surely the dull, monotonous life of "religious communities" like the Moravians, Shakers, Rappites and others find followers; why not this bright, happy, cheering, frank life of ours?

We are expecting a visit from Horace Greeley soon; I have never seen him, but we have heaps of strangers coming every day, some quite distinguished and some plain folks, but the average are wide-awake people.

Truly your friend,
John C. Foster

Discussion: Does it take a particular kind of person to commit to being part of an idealistic community like Brook Farm? If you lived at that time, would you have been drawn to such an experience?

Connecting with Our Lives

In Our Faith Communities
In 1837, George Ripley observed that "the inordinate pursuit, the extravagant worship of wealth" was a great danger to our country. Is this still true today? Here are some possible topics for discussion in small groups, youth groups, or covenant groups:

- Invite participants to discuss whether there are things of great value that money can't buy, and if so, what they are and how we nurture these values.
- Encourage participants to reflect on how we, as individuals, think about our relationship to wealth, whether as a goal, a means to an end, a primary concern, or a secondary concern. Explore the extent to which the pursuit of wealth or anxiety about financial concerns rule our lives.
- Have participants consider whether socialistic schemes invariably result in loss of individual rights, as many people fear. Analyze Brook Farm's ideal of a cooperative society that exists for the purpose, as Sophia Ripley said, of providing "a healthier atmosphere" that "may furnish a better chance for vigorous growth" of each individual, and evaluate that ideal as realistic or not.

At Home

If you could design the ideal school or intentional community, what would it be like? The following questions might help you begin:

- What ideals would be at the center of your community?
- To what extent would competition be encouraged, and to what ends?
- What would be the balance of intellectual and physical work?
- How important would amusements be, and how would they be planned?
- How integrated or separate would the community be from the everyday world?

Draw, paint, or write about your ideal community, and share your work with others in your family, or work together on designing your ideal community. What aspects of your design might you incorporate into your family life right now, even if you don't go on to actualize all of what you envision? Remember, this is your personal ideal—your "castle in the air." Who knows where it might lead? As Henry David Thoreau writes in *Walden*, "If you have built castles in the air, your work need not be lost; that is where they should be. Now put the foundations under them."

Find Out More

Buell, Lawrence. *The American Transcendentalists: Essential Writings.* New York: Modern Library, 2006.

Codman, John Thomas. *Brook Farm: Historic and Personal Memoirs.* Boston: Arena Publishing, 1894. It can be read online at Google Books.

Cooke, George Willis. "Brook Farm." *The New England Magazine* 17, no. 4 (December 1897): 391–407. It can be read online at the digital library of Cornell University.

Gura, Philip F. *American Transcendentalism: A History.* New York: Hill and Wang, 2007.

Raymond, Henrietta Dana. *Sophia Willard Dana Ripley, Co-Founder of Brook Farm.* Portsmouth, NH: Peter E. Randall Publisher, 1994.

Robinson, David. "George Ripley." *Dictionary of Unitarian and Universalist Biography*, published online by the Unitarian Universalist Historical Society at www25.uua.org/uuhs.

Sears, John Van der Zee. *My Friends at Brook Farm.* New York: Desmond FitzGerald, 1912. It can be read online at Project Gutenberg or Google Books.

Swift, Lindsay. *Brook Farm: Its Members, Scholars, and Visitors.* An exact, unabridged, and unaltered reprint of the original publication in 1900. Secaucus, NJ: Citadel Press, 1973. It can be read online at Google Books.

Abolition of Slavery

Lydia Maria Child Battles Racism with Her Pen

People today may think that most Northerners favored abolition of slavery in the years before the Civil War, but in fact, the vast majority of Americans—in the North as well as the South—despised and reviled abolitionists. The practice of slavery had long been controversial, but the United States Constitution officially recognized its legality. By 1820, slavery had been largely eliminated in the Northern states while Southern states remained fully committed to a system of slave labor. Most Northerners remained silent on the subject, even if they considered the practice of slavery morally repugnant. Since their own economy depended on trade with the South, they defended the status quo to avoid disrupting people's livelihoods. Most people viewed abolitionists not as humanitarians but as troublemakers who were threatening to destabilize the country.

Lydia Maria Child (1802–1880) was one Northerner who was willing to take a courageous and dedicated stand against slavery, even though it meant giving up a promising career. Born Lydia Francis in Medford, Massachusetts, she was the youngest child of a baker. As a girl, she had very little schooling. Her development as an intellectual and a highly respected writer owed much to her brother, Convers Francis, Jr., who was older by six years. He was a brilliant young scholar who obtained a Harvard education despite his family's lack of money and social standing. Convers Francis became a Unitarian minister and a member of the Transcendentalist circle. He encouraged his sister's voracious appetite for learning by giving her access to his library, as well as opportunities to discuss literature and ideas. In 1821, when he became minister of the Unitarian Church in Watertown, Massachusetts, his sister joined his household. It was around this time that she asked people to use her middle name, Maria, in preference to Lydia.

Maria Francis Child admired her brother very much, but she never fully embraced his religious views. She remained a spiritual seeker, hoping to find a religion that would nourish her soul. William Ellery Channing's preaching may have come closest to her ideal, but she was frustrated by his lack of commitment to the antislavery cause. On that issue, Child did have an impact on him. Her book An Appeal in Favor of That Class of Americans Called Africans (1833) *was the first and most comprehensive antislavery book published in America. After reading it, Channing was moved to publish his own ideas on this highly charged topic. Although his condemnation of slavery was mild and equivocal compared with hers, his words brought the issue to the attention of many Unitarians who would have ignored an outright abolitionist like Child, and helped bring sympathy to the antislavery cause.*

Channing admired Child, but her position was too radical for him and for most Unitarians of the time. A commitment to the antislavery cause had swept over her forcibly, very much like a religious conversion, and reform had become her religion. Lydia Maria Child, a true believer in racial equality, tried to move the United States toward her vision of a multiracial egalitarian society at a time when most whites—even antislavery whites—took for granted their own racial superiority.

Imagine a housewife in the 1820s, an energetic young woman very capable in the arts of sewing, cooking, and housekeeping. Imagine that this young housewife is also a popular novelist and the editor of America's first successful children's magazine. Her literary accomplishments have made her a welcome guest in the drawing rooms of Boston's elite society, but her recent marriage has put her in a bit of a bind. Her husband is an idealist who seems incapable of earning a living. She is struggling to maintain a household on little more than ingenuity and hard work. What can she do? Why, write a book about it, of course!

Now picture a fiercely independent young woman who refuses to bow to nineteenth-century ideals of womanhood. She expresses her beliefs publicly, even when she knows that most people do not share them. She believes, for example, that American Indians and Africans are born with the same capabilities as Europeans and that they are equally beloved by God. The more she learns about the way Native people and Africans have been treated in the United States, the more determined she is to speak out in their defense. She turns her pen into a sword of truth, writing books, stories, and magazine articles aimed at demolishing racial prejudice. She will not let the sneers of proper Bostonians silence her. She will work tirelessly for the abolition of slavery, even though she knows this will make her unpopular, both in the North, where she lives, and in the South, where slavery still exists.

Would it surprise you to learn that these two women are actually one person? Her name was Lydia Maria Child.

The first description is of Child in 1829, when she was twenty-seven years old. The book she wrote that year was called *The Frugal Housewife*. It was an advice manual filled with useful information and tips about how to manage a household when money is scarce. The book became one of the most popular and valued books in America. Numerous editions were published over the next few years, and thousands of copies were sold. She followed it with *The Mother's Book* and *The Little Girl's Own Book*. It seemed there was an insatiable appetite for Child's advice, not just in America but in England, Scotland, and Germany as well. In the words of the *North American Review*, an important literary journal, "We are not sure that any woman in our country would outrank Mrs. Child. This lady has long been before the public as an author, with much success. And she well deserves it,—for in all her works we think that nothing can be found, which does not commend itself."

It would not be long, though, before the literary journals in America would sing a very different tune. A year after she published *The Frugal Housewife*, Child met the fiery young abolitionist William Lloyd Garrison. His words fanned a flame in her soul that had already been glowing. For many years, messages about racial justice had found their way into her children's stories and novels. Now she resolved to commit herself wholeheartedly to the cause of ending slavery.

She still had a lot of questions. Was immediate emancipation—freeing all slaves at once—the best way? Her husband David thought so, as did William Lloyd Garrison, but she was not sure. The Boston newspapers said that abolitionists were dangerous fanatics. People in the South claimed that if the slaves were freed, they would brutally murder their former masters. The Colonization Society argued that the best solution was to free slaves gradually and transport them to Africa. Child wanted to know what was right. She began a thorough study of slavery throughout the world. Then she published what she learned in a book that addressed the controversy in all its aspects: historical, moral, economic, legal, and political.

An Appeal in Favor of That Class of Americans Called Africans appeared in 1833. The title was awkward, but it sent an important message. Blacks in America were as American as anybody else. The idea of sending free blacks to Africa was an unworkable scheme born of racial prejudice.

Child's *Appeal* was well researched, skillfully argued, and written in language that anyone could understand. Her findings were clear: Slavery was cruel and inhumane. It degraded the character of the slaveholder as much as the slave. Emancipation would reduce the risk of violence, not increase it. She pointed out that racial injustice was by no means limited to the slave-holding states. Northerners were also to blame. They participated in the slave economy and treated free blacks unfairly. "Let us no longer act upon the narrow idea, that we must always continue to do wrong, because we have so long been in the habit of doing it," she urged.

The public was outraged. They did not want to hear this from any writer, much less from a woman. Parents cancelled their subscriptions to Child's popular children's magazine. Sales of her advice books plummeted. People who had formerly befriended her now shunned her.

Lydia Maria Child's life would never be the same. She had made more enemies than friends. But the *Appeal* did make her popular among a small group of antislavery activists—a group whose numbers were growing because of her book.

The fact that Child was already a famous author lent power to her pen. People might have disagreed with her, but they did pay attention to what she had to say. In verbal exchanges with proslavery writers, Child scored many victories. She was especially good at pointing out inconsistencies in proslavery positions. If blacks had inferior minds, with little capacity for learning, why would the slave states need to impose such heavy penalties on all who attempted to give blacks an education? If blacks were happier in bondage than free, why would so many slaves risk all to run away? And why would slaveholders grant freedom as a reward instead of a punishment?

The Civil War abolished slavery at last, but Lydia Maria Child knew that only half the battle had been won. How could people who had been forbidden to read, to express themselves, or to have homes and families of their own now become productive and responsible citizens? In 1865, she published *The Freedmen's Book*, a collection of poems, stories, and advice designed both to educate the newly freed population and to encourage pride and self-confidence. She included biographies of famous black people, along with many selections written by black authors and poets. When she learned that the wages of former slaves kept them too poor to purchase a book, Child put nearly every penny she could earn into printing and distributing it.

Ralph Waldo Emerson once wrote, "Conservatism goes for comfort, reform for truth." For this ever-frugal housewife, going for comfort now would have been like steering her ship toward an alien shore. Reform and truth were the true north of her conscience, and she stayed on course to the end.

Quotations for Discussion

Even before she became involved in the antislavery cause, Lydia Maria Child quietly advocated for American Indian rights. Her first book, *Hobomok*, published when she was just twenty-two years old, tells the tale of a marriage between an American Indian of noble character and an English settler. Although some considered the notion of interracial marriage distasteful (especially from the pen of an unmarried woman!), the novel was well reviewed and established the author's fame. In 1828, as the Cherokees and other Civilized Tribes of the South were threatened with removal from their lands (a threat later carried out), Child took up the Native American theme again. In *The First Settlers of New-England*, she traces the cruel treatment of Native Americans to the actions and beliefs of the Puritans. The keen insight into human psychology that became a hallmark of her antislavery campaign was already in evidence. She portrays the Indians as people engaged in a patriotic struggle for their rights, while the Puritans used religious justifications to slaughter them. A mother explains to her daughters the complex workings of the Calvinist religion on Puritan minds, saying,

> A sect who ascribe to their God passions highly vindictive and unjust . . . may have believed themselves authorized to inflict all the evil in their power on wretches who are born to suffer. . . .
>
> However strong were their convictions of the justice of their cause, however plausible were their arguments in defence of their usurpations, they were unable to silence the voice of conscience; and they vainly attempted to escape from the remorse, which, with all its terrors, seizes on the hearts of the guilty, by redoubling their superstitious observances. They fasted and prayed, and the austerities they imposed on themselves and others destroyed in a great degree all social enjoyment; and whilst they were systematically planning the destruction of the Indians, they were sharply engaged in discussing with each other points of

faith altogether unimportant or incomprehensible.... People seldom forgive those whom they have wronged, and the first settlers appear to have fostered a mortal aversion to the Indians, whom they had barbarously destroyed.

Discussion: What contemporary applications do you see of Child's insight about the role of guilt in the actions and attitudes of a group who has wronged or oppressed another?

֍

At William Lloyd Garrison's death, Child wrote of her first meeting with him in 1830,

> I little thought then that the whole pattern of my life-web would be changed by that introduction. I was then all absorbed in poetry and painting,—soaring aloft, on Psyche-wings, into the ethereal regions of mysticism. He got hold of the strings of my conscience, and pulled me into Reforms. It is of no use to imagine what might have been, if I had never met him. Old dreams vanished, old associates departed, and all things became new.... A new stimulus seized my whole being, and carried me whithersoever it would.

Discussion: Child describes a conversion experience that led her to dedicate her life to working for social justice and equality. Describe a similar conversion story of your own—an event, a person, or a chance meeting that gave you a new sense of purpose and meaning.

֍

The following are excerpts from *An Appeal in Favor of That Class of Americans Called Africans* (1833):

> And now let us briefly inquire into the influence of slavery on the white man's character; for in this evil there is a mighty

re-action. "Such is the constitution of things, that we cannot inflict an injury without suffering from it ourselves; he who blesses another, benefits himself; but he, who sins against his fellow creature, does his own soul a grievous wrong."

In a community where all the labor is done by one class, there must of course be another class, who live in indolence; and we all know how much people that have nothing to do are tempted by what the world calls pleasures; the result is, that slave-holding states and colonies are proverbial for dissipation. Hence too the contempt for industry, which prevails in such a state of society. Where none work but slaves, usefulness becomes degradation.

Among the other apologies for slavery, it has been asserted that the Bible does not forbid it. Neither does it forbid the counterfeiting of a bank-bill. It is the spirit of the Holy Word, not its particular expressions, which must be a rule for our conduct. How can slavery be reconciled with the maxim, "Do unto others, as ye would that others should do unto you."?

Slavery is so inconsistent with free institutions, and the spirit of liberty is so contagious under such institutions, that the system must either be given up, or sustained by laws outrageously severe; hence we find that our slave laws have each year been growing more harsh than those of any other nation. . . . Shall I be told that all these regulations are necessary for the white man's safety? What then, let me indignantly ask, what must the system be that requires to be supported by such unnatural, such tyrannical means! The very apology pronounces the condemnation of slavery—for it proves that it cannot exist without producing boundless misery to the oppressed, and perpetual terror to the oppressor.

It is a favorite argument that we are not to blame for slavery, because the British engrafted it upon us, while we were colonies. But did we not take the liberty to change English laws and customs, when they did not suit us? Why not put away this, as well as other evils of much less consequence? . . .

The plain truth is, the continuation of this system is a sin; and the sin rests upon us; It has been eloquently said that "by this excuse, we try to throw the blame upon our ancestors, and leave repentance to posterity."

Discussion: What do Child's arguments against slavery tell us about the prevailing social understandings of her day? Discuss any of her arguments that may have echoes in contemporary political debates.

⑥

Lydia Maria Child offered aid to the imprisoned abolitionist John Brown after his failed raid at Harper's Ferry (1859). Her letter to him became public, and an exchange of letters between Child and Margaretta Mason, wife of Virginia's Senator James M. Mason, followed. Mrs. Mason opened with the rebuke, "Do you read your Bible, Mrs. Child? If you do, read there, 'Woe unto you, hypocrites.'" She accused Child of ignoring the Northern white poor and confining her sympathy to a man who had sought to unleash a "servile war" against the men, women, and children of her own race. Mrs. Mason urged Child to take a lesson in true charity from the slave-holding women of the South:

> Would you stand by the bedside of an old negro, dying of a hopeless disease, to alleviate his sufferings as far as human aid could? . . . Do you soften the pangs of maternity in those around you by all the care and comfort you can give? . . . Did you ever sit up until the "wee hours" to complete a dress for a motherless child, that she might appear on Christmas day in a new one?

Child answered in an eleven-page letter. She began with an array of biblical texts: eighteen quotes supporting an antislavery interpretation of Christianity, compared with the two Mason had found for slavery. She then urged Mason to consider the many benefits the South would derive from emancipation. Finally she addressed the questions Mrs. Mason had raised about practical good works:

> It would be extremely difficult to find any woman in our villages who does *not* sew for the poor, and watch with the sick, whenever occasion requires. We pay our domestics generous wages, with which they can purchase as many Christmas gowns as they please; a process far better for their characters, as well as our own, than to receive their clothing as a charity, after being deprived of just payment for their labor. I have never known an instance where the "pangs of maternity" did not meet with requisite assistance; and here at the North, after we have helped the mothers, *we do not sell the babies.*

Discussion: What insights does this exchange of letters offer into the cultural differences that contributed to the American Civil War?

Connecting with Our Lives

In Our Faith Communities

Lydia Maria Child's life brings us face-to-face with questions about our own relationship to social action. She was willing to give up the approval she had earned—willing to become a virtual outcast from society—not because she had to, but because working to right the world's wrongs had become more important to her than popularity or material comfort. She didn't shrink from writing about subjects that others considered taboo, even though her outspokenness on the subject of slavery put an end to her promising career. Her commitment to ending slavery, along with her marriage to an idealistic but impractical reformer, brought her financial hardship and a lifetime of household drudgery. How many of us would be willing to make such a sacrifice?

On the other hand, Child's activism brought her into a circle of other committed reformers who admired her and whom she admired. It gave her a faith to which she could devote a lifetime of good works and the satisfaction of accomplishing something important. As an outcast of society, she gained the freedom to speak her mind without the encumbrances of nineteenth-century respectability.

Invite small groups to consider your congregation's work on behalf of social justice through the lens of Lydia Maria Child's life and work. Ask them to think about the rewards the congregation finds in committing some portion of your lives and material wealth to social action. Consider together whether there is any cost to the congregation when you defend unpopular causes. Examine what core beliefs you would be willing to defend, even if it means asking congregants to make personal sacrifices, to forfeit social standing, or even to risk reprisal.

At Home

Before Lydia Maria Child fully committed herself to the abolitionist cause, she researched the subject of slavery extensively. At a deep level, she believed slavery to be wrong, but even among those who opposed slavery, there were differing opinions about how to end it—along with a vast sea of prejudices and fears. She considered each argument for or against abolition in light of the facts she learned, and decided for herself which course seemed to be most clearly grounded in the truth. Armed with the truth as she could best discover it, she then took decisive action.

Others were not so scrupulous about the truth. After the publication of some of Lydia Maria Child's antislavery arguments in the Southern press, a New Orleans newspaper correspondent planted a false story, claiming that Child had abandoned a crippled daughter who was being generously supported by a Mississippi slaveholder. Lydia Maria Child had no children and would most certainly never have abandoned any person for whom she was responsible—yet this story was picked up and widely circulated by proslavery newspapers throughout the country.

As Unitarian Universalists, we believe that standing up for truth is important, although it is not always easy. Most of us are quick to believe stories that confirm our prejudices and beliefs. False claims can be powerful, and the more they are repeated, the harder it is to debunk them. Harmful rumors and claims can destroy the success of a person or a cause, even after they are proven false.

With your family, consider what value you place on truth. Make a list together of how you can guard against believing or spreading false claims. Talk about how verifying facts and valuing truth applies to schoolyard or neighborhood gossip as much as to people and events in the news.

Find Out More

Child, Lydia Maria Francis. *An Appeal in Favor of That Class of Americans Called Africans*, Bedford, MA: Applewood Books, 1833. It can be read online at Google Books.

———. *Anti-Slavery Catechism*. Newburyport, MA: Charles Whipple, 1839. It can be read online at www.archive.org.

———. *The Freedmen's Book*. Boston: Ticknor and Fields, 1865. It can be read online at Google Books.

Clifford, Deborah Pickman. *Crusader for Freedom: A Life of Lydia Maria Child*. Boston: Beacon Press, 1992.

Goodwin, Joan. "Lydia Maria Child." *Dictionary of Unitarian and Universalist Biography*, published online by the Unitarian Universalist Historical Society at www25.uua.org/uuhs.

Karcher, Carolyn L. *The First Woman in the Republic: A Cultural Biography of Lydia Maria Child*. Durham, NC: Duke University Press, 1994.

Meltzer, Milton. *Tongue of Flame: The Life of Lydia Maria Child*. New York: Thomas Y. Crowell, 1965.

Antislavery Poet and Orator Frances Ellen Watkins Harper

Lydia Maria Child wrote about racial equality, using true stories to convince her readers that blacks and whites had equal abilities and a common humanity. Frances Ellen Watkins Harper (1825–1911) could go one step further. As a free black woman who was a talented public speaker and writer, she bore witness to the truth of Child's claim just by being herself. From her first public speech in 1854 through the end of the century, Harper was a public advocate for social reforms. In the early years, abolition was her major concern. After emancipation, she became well known as a supporter of temperance and women's rights. She often spoke to audiences of former slaves, instructing them in the values and skills they would need to become independent and successful. She is not well known today, but her poetry, essays, and speeches were very popular in her own time. Not surprisingly, Lydia Maria Child included several poems by Harper in The Freedmen's Book.

Frances Ellen Watkins Harper belonged to a Unitarian church in her later years. Scholars who have studied her life and work assert that she was a lifelong Unitarian, although she also participated in activities of the African Methodist Episcopal Church. From her earliest writings on religion, it is clear that Harper's Christian faith was founded on intellect and reason. She emphasized personal responsibility and believed that social transformation depended upon elevating the moral conscience of individuals. This faith was at the heart of her reform efforts.

Harper published at least seven volumes of poetry during her lifetime, as well as lectures, essays, and several works of fiction. In 1871, black activist William Still reported that "fifty thousand copies at least of her four small books have been sold to those who have listened to her eloquent lectures." She was the leading African American poet of the nineteenth century, but after her death, she was all but forgotten. No doubt, this was partly due to the fact that her writing was very specific to the issues of her day. She wanted to influence history by changing people's minds and hearts. She reached large audiences by keeping her writing in tune to the popular taste of the time—a style later regarded as overly didactic. In the 1960s, scholars began to rediscover and reprint her work, giving us the chance today to appreciate the skill and courage of this remarkable writer and reformer.

In the city of Philadelphia, Pennsylvania, in the year 1858, a young woman entered a streetcar and sat down. The conductor came to her and insisted she leave, but she stayed quietly in her seat. A passenger intervened, asking if the woman in question might be permitted to sit in a corner. She did not move. When she reached her destination, the woman got up and tried to pay the fare, but the conductor refused to take her money. She threw it down on the floor and left.

What was that all about?

It was all about racism. The white conductor was giving the woman on the streetcar a hard time because she was African American, and Frances Ellen Watkins was having none of it. She believed in equality. She believed in treating all people with dignity and respect. Her work obliged her to travel from place to place, and she was used to enduring prejudice and injustice. She had the courage not to let it stop her.

Frances Ellen Watkins was born in 1825 in Maryland, when slavery was still legal. Born to free parents, she was never a slave. But by the age of three, she was an orphan, living with relatives in Baltimore. Her sad situation had one fortunate outcome. Her uncle William Watkins ran a school called the Academy for Negro Youth, and Frances received an excellent classical education there. Such schools for blacks were very rare.

By the age of fourteen, Frances had to leave school and go to work. She became a domestic servant. But this unfortunate situation also offered an opportunity. The Quaker family she worked for owned a bookshop and also had books in the house. Whenever time allowed, they gave her free access to all those books. She was an avid reader and soon became known as a writer too. By the age of twenty, she had written enough poems and essays to publish a small book.

Life for free blacks in Maryland was difficult and became worse after the Fugitive Slave Act of 1850. William Watkins was forced to close his school. He moved to Canada with some of the family, but Frances, at age twenty-five, moved to the free state of Ohio, where she took a job teaching sewing. Two years later, she moved to Pennsylvania, where she continued to teach. Her heart told her that educating black children was the most important work in the world, but she soon realized that managing fifty-three unruly pupils in rural Pennsylvania was not the right job for her.

While she considered what to do next, events in her home state gave her a new aspiration. Maryland passed a law saying that any free person of color who entered the state would be arrested and sold into slavery. Frances Watkins heard about a young man who unwittingly crossed into Maryland and was sold to a Georgia slaveholder. He escaped but was recaptured and sent back to Georgia, where he soon died. "Upon that grave," Watkins wrote to a friend, "I pledged myself to the Anti-Slavery cause."

Watkins moved to Philadelphia, where there was a substantial community of well-educated and successful blacks. Homeless and friendless, she found her way to William Still, a leader in the African American community. Still was chairman of the Vigilance Committee, organized to assist runaway slaves passing through Philadelphia. His home was the busiest station on the Underground Railroad—a place where people fleeing from slavery could rest and find assistance. Watkins met many fugitives there and heard their heartrending stories.

For Watkins, the antislavery cause opened a whole new career. Abolitionist papers began publishing her work, and in 1854, she gave a public lecture on "The Education and the Elevation of the Colored Race." She gave several more lectures that same week, and soon she had a full-time job as a traveling lecturer for the State Anti-Slavery Society of Maine. She drew large audiences, and judging from newspaper accounts and reviews, she did not disappoint them. New Englanders had long disapproved of women who spoke in public, but opinions were beginning to change, and Frances Watkins was a novelty. Audiences, whether black or white, male or female, wanted to hear this eloquent woman of color who outshone nearly all other orators on the circuit. They were charmed by her musical voice, her well-reasoned arguments, and her poetic language. She published a book of poems in 1854, and thousands of people who attended her lectures bought her book after hearing her speak.

She donated most of the money she earned from her books to the antislavery cause. Whenever she could, she sent a few dollars to William Still for the Vigilance Committee and the fugitives. At one point, he must have admonished Watkins to keep more of her earnings for herself. She wrote back, "Let me explain a few matters to you. In the first place, I am able to give something. In the second place, I am willing to do so." In fact, she was more than willing and able. To her, helping humanity was a sacred calling, and she felt blessed to be able to do it. "Oh, is it not a privilege," she wrote to a friend, "if you are sisterless and lonely, to be a sister to the human race, and to place your heart where it may throb close to downtrodden humanity?"

Watkins supported a movement called Free Produce, which encouraged people to boycott all products tied to slave labor. "Oh, could slavery exist long if it did not sit on a commercial throne?" she wrote. "Our moral influence against slavery must be weakened, our testimony diluted if . . . we are constantly demanding rice from the swamps, cotton from the plantations and sugar from the deadly mills."

She hoped that blacks would establish a network of schools, newspapers, and churches dedicated to the betterment of themselves and each other. She believed that an important goal of antislavery work was to teach her people "how to build up a character for themselves—a character that will challenge respect in spite of opposition and prejudice; to develop their own souls, intellect and genius, and thus verify their credentials."

In 1860, Frances Ellen Watkins married Fenton Harper. When war broke out between the North and the South, she was living on a small farm in Ohio. But her husband died after less than four years of marriage, leaving Frances with a little daughter. She returned to the lecture circuit and traveled throughout the North, supporting the war effort and encouraging the Union Army to allow black troops to join them in the fight.

The Civil War ended slavery in America, leaving blacks with great hopes but also enormous problems. Frances Harper continued to give speeches and lectures, working in the South now, as well as the North. She did all she could to defend, support, and educate the newly freed blacks.

Frances Harper advocated for equality and reforms for the rest of her life. The racist rhetoric of her day was ugly, and white people who harmed or even murdered blacks usually went unpunished, yet she did not give in to anger or despair. Her words helped Americans across racial lines understand their common humanity and common yearnings. She believed she could contribute to the betterment of society by uplifting her listeners, and she hoped that her life might "gladden the earth." She shone a light on injustice so that others might see it more clearly—but she remained confident that someday, there would be liberty and justice for all.

Quotations for Discussion

In a letter to William Still (1859), Frances Ellen Watkins writes, "The nearer we ally ourselves to the wants and woes of humanity in the spirit of Christ, the closer we get to the great heart of God; the nearer we stand by the beating of the pulse of universal love."

She had earlier written an essay called "Christianity" (1853) that explained the beliefs at the heart of her lifetime commitment to serving humanity. The following excerpts from that essay highlight ways in which religion provided both her guiding principles and a needed solace:

> Christianity is a system claiming God for its author, and the welfare of man for its object. It is a system so uniform, exalted and pure, that the loftiest intellects have acknowledged its influence, and acquiesced in the justness of its claims. . . . The constant friend of man, she has stood by him in his hour of greatest need. She has cheered the prisoner in his cell, and strengthened the martyr at the stake. She has nerved the frail and shrinking heart of woman for high and holy deeds. The worn and weary have rested their fainting heads upon her bosom, and gathered strength from her words and courage from her counsels. . . .
>
> Christianity has changed the moral aspect of nations. . . . At her approach, fetters have been broken, and men have risen redeemed from dust, and freed from chains. Manhood has learned its dignity and worth; its kindred with angels, and alliance to God. . . .
>
> Amid ancient lore the Word of God stands unique and pre-eminent. . . . It addresses itself to [man's] moral and spiritual nature, makes provision for his wants and weaknesses, and meets his yearnings and aspirations. It is adapted to his mind in its earliest stages of progression, and its highest state of intellectuality. It provides light for his darkness, joy for his anguish, a solace for his woes, balm for his wounds, and heaven for his hopes. . . . Aided by the Holy Spirit, it guides us through life, points out the shoals, the quicksands and hidden rocks which endanger our path, and at last leaves us with the eternal God for our refuge, and his everlasting arms for our protection.

Discussion: Why might Watkins personify Christianity as a feminine entity? From the images in the essay, what would you say about the kind of comfort Christian faith provided to this woman, who was orphaned as a young child and widowed after less than four years of marriage? How did it help her comfort others?

❦

On May 13, 1857, Frances Ellen Watkins addressed the New York Anti-Slavery Society. This speech, later printed in the *National Anti-Slavery Standard*, is believed to be the only surviving example of her antislavery lectures. Here are two excerpts from that address:

> A hundred thousand newborn babes are annually added to the victims of slavery; twenty thousand lives are annually sacrificed on the plantations of the South. Such a sight should send a thrill of horror through the nerves of civilization and impel the heart of humanity to lofty deeds. So it might, if men had not found out a fearful alchemy by which this blood can be transformed into gold. Instead of listening to the cry of agony, they listen to the ring of dollars and stoop down to pick up the coin. . . .
>
> But I will not dwell on the dark side of the picture. God is on the side of freedom; and any cause that has God on its side, I care not how much it may be trampled upon, how much it may be trailed in the dust, is sure to triumph. The message of Jesus Christ is on the side of freedom, "I come to preach deliverance to the captives, the opening of the prison doors to them that are bound." The truest and noblest hearts in the land are on the side of freedom. They may be hissed at by slavery's minions, their names cast out as evil, their characters branded with fanaticism, but O, "To side with Truth is noble when we share her humble crust Ere the cause bring fame and profit and it's prosperous to be just."
>
> May I not, in conclusion, ask every honest, noble heart, every seeker after truth and justice, if they will not also be on the side of freedom. Will you not resolve that you will abate neither heart nor hope till you hear the death-knell

of human bondage sounded, and over the black ocean of slavery shall be heard a song, more exulting than the song of Miriam when it floated o'er Egypt's dark sea, the requiem of Egypt's ruined hosts and the anthem of the deliverance of Israel's captive people?

Discussion: Watkins' antislavery words appealed to important cultural and religious values in her listeners, invoking powerful metaphors and rhetorical phrases. What values and metaphors today are persuasive in advocating for justice? What is the role of oratory in galvanizing hearts and minds in support of a cause?

In a letter to William Still (October 20, 1854), Frances Ellen Watkins expressed her dedication to the principle of avoiding goods produced by slave labor:

> I have reason to be thankful that I am able to give a little more for a Free Labor dress, if it is coarser. I can thank God that upon its warp and woof I see no stain of blood and tears; that to procure a little finer muslin for my limbs no crushed and broken heart went out in sighs, and that from the field in which it was raised went up no wild and startling cry unto the throne of God to witness there in language deep and strong, that in demanding that cotton I was nerving oppression's hand for deeds of guilt and crime.

Later, she used many of those same words in her poem "Free Labor" that would help to create public sympathy for the cause:

> I wear an easy garment,
>   O'er it no toiling slave
> Wept tears of hopeless anguish,
>   In his passage to the grave.

And from its ample folds
    Shall rise no cry to God,
Upon its warp and woof shall be
    No stain of tears and blood.

Oh, Lightly shall it press my form,
    Unladened with a sigh,
I shall not 'mid its rustling hear,
    Some sad despairing cry.

This fabric is too light to bear
    The weight of bondsmen's tears,
I shall not in its texture trace
    The agony of years.

Too light to bear a smother'd sigh,
    From some lorn woman's heart,
Whose only wreath of household love
    Is rudely torn apart.

Then lightly shall it press my form,
    Unburden'd by a sigh;
And from its seams and folds shall rise,
    No voice to pierce the sky,

And witness at the throne of God,
    In language deep and strong,
That I have nerv'd Oppression's hand,
    For deeds of guilt and wrong.

Discussion: What other historic and contemporary justice movements have employed a strategy similar to Frances Ellen Watkins Harper's? Have you ever joined in a boycott of goods or services so as not to support oppression? How easy or difficult did you find it to honor such a commitment?

It is amazing that Frances Watkins Harper attracted such large and appreciative audiences. When viewed from our twenty-first century perspective, the attitudes of many whites toward black people seem unbelievably repugnant. Professor Thomas Dew of Virginia wrote that free blacks "must be considered the most worthless and indolent of the citizens of the United States. It is well known that throughout the whole extent of our Union, they are looked upon as the very *drones* and *pests* of society." The powerful statesman John C. Calhoun of South Carolina gave a speech in the Senate arguing that slavery is actually good for black people. "Never before has the black race of Central Africa, from the dawn of history to the present day, attained a condition so civilized and so improved." Senator Hammond agreed. "None of that race on the whole face of the globe can be compared with the slaves of the South," he claimed. "They are happy, content, unaspiring, and utterly incapable, from intellectual weakness, ever to give us any trouble by their aspirations."

The impression Frances Harper made on the public was a strong counterbalance to prevailing stereotypes. A reviewer in the *Christian Recorder*, on May 21, 1864, wrote, "Seldom have we heard a more cogent, forcible, and eloquent lecture upon any subject, especially from a woman." And Phebe Hanaford, a Universalist minister and feminist, wrote in 1882,

> Frances E. W. Harper is one of the most eloquent women lecturers in the country. As one listens to her clear, plaintive, melodious voice, and follows the flow of her musical speech in her logical presentation of the truth, he can but be charmed by her oratory and rhetoric, and forgets she is of the race once enslaved in our land.

Discussion: What might be the ongoing cultural, economic, or social legacy of prevailing attitudes toward African Americans? While it is easy to condemn the words of people like Calhoun, how do you respond to the friendlier words, which also reveal gender and racial prejudice?

Connecting with Our Lives

In Our Faith Communities

Slavery still exists in many guises today. In the United States, it is likely that at some time we all unwittingly use products that have been produced by slave labor. The problem is hard to track in a global economy. It may be that one component of a complex electronic device you own was produced by slave labor. It may be that some percentage of the cacao used in a brand of chocolate you like comes from plantations that use slave labor. Frances Ellen Watkins Harper's support for free labor is paralleled in today's Fair Trade movement. In her poem "Free Labor," she points out that she would rather pay more for goods made without slave labor than have a slave's agony on her conscience.

Invite your congregation to find out how you can promote awareness of slavery and avoidance of slave-produced goods and to research other unfair labor practices. Investigate your purchasing as a congregation to discover whether you buy and serve Fair Trade coffee and tea. Discuss what other actions you might take to make sure you aren't supporting the use of slave labor.

At Home

Frances Ellen Watkins Harper used poetry as a means of communicating important ideas in a way that would touch people's hearts. Think of a social issue that is important to you. Try writing about it in two ways: first, in prose, as in Harper's letter to William Still, and then in a poem. Which way of communicating has more power for you?

Find Out More

Grohsmeyer, Janeen. "Frances Harper." *Dictionary of Unitarian and Universalist Biography*, published online by the Unitarian Universalist Historical Society at www25.uua.org/uuhs.

Hanaford, Phebe A. *Daughters of America*. Augusta, ME: True and Co., 1882. It can be read online at Google Books.

Harper, Frances Ellen Watkins. *A Brighter Coming Day: A Frances Ellen Watkins Harper Reader*, ed. and introd. Frances Smith Foster. New York: The Feminist Press, 1990.

———. *Iola Leroy, or Shadows Uplifted*, introd. Frances Smith Foster. New York: Oxford University Press, 1988. It can be read online at Google Books.

———. *Minnie's Sacrifice, Sowing and Reaping, Trial and Triumph: Three Rediscovered Novels*, ed. and introd. Frances Smith Foster. Boston: Beacon Press, 1994.

Peterson, Carla L. *"Doers of the Word": African-American Women Speakers & Writers in the North (1830–1880)*. New Brunswick, NJ: Rutgers University Press, 1995.

Sterling, Dorothy, ed. *We Are Your Sisters: Black Women in the Nineteenth Century.* New York: W. W. Norton, 1984.

Still, William. *The Underground Rail Road*. Philadelphia: Porters and Coates, 1872. It can be read online at the Dickinson College Digital Collections.

Theodore Parker and the Fugitive Slave Law

Theodore Parker (1810–1860) was one of the best-known and most controversial Unitarian ministers of the nineteenth century. He was an eloquent speaker, a scholar with an impressive breadth and depth of knowledge, and a member of the Transcendentalist circle. He was minister of the church in West Roxbury, Massachusetts, from 1837 to 1846, and residents of the nearby Brook Farm community often came to hear him preach.

In 1846, the newly formed Twenty-eighth Congregational Society of Boston chose Parker as their minister, and by 1852, about two thousand people were attending his weekly services, held in the Boston Music Hall. Parker was well known for his theological disputes with mainstream Unitarians in the early 1840s, but he was not associated with the antislavery cause until the time of the Mexican War, which followed the Annexation of Texas in 1845. Like Thoreau, who was jailed for his refusal to pay taxes for that war (the event that inspired his famous essay, "Civil Disobedience"), Parker believed that the people of Massachusetts should not participate in a proslavery expansionist war. Parker began to compare the tyranny of the "Slave Power" with the tyranny of England before the Revolution, calling for a second great struggle for the principles of liberty and independence. Unlike William Lloyd Garrison and some of the other leading abolitionists, he did not oppose the use of violence in defending liberty.

Passage of the Fugitive Slave Law of 1850 forced Parker to dedicate himself more fully to the antislavery cause. Abiding by that law would have obliged him to participate in the kidnapping of fugitive slaves and free blacks, some of whom were his own parishioners, and he was determined to defy it. By the end of 1850, Parker was devoting much of his time to the Boston Committee for Safety and Vigilance, of which he was a cofounder and leader.

This is the story of Theodore Parker, a Unitarian minister who was determined to do whatever he could to end slavery in the United States. His powerful sermons were legendary. This is also the story of Millard Fillmore, whose actions earned him the contempt of Theodore Parker and abolitionists everywhere. He became the president of the United States in 1850.

But the story begins with a married couple from Macon, Georgia, who planned a daring escape from slavery. Ellen Craft had skin so light that she could easily pass for white. She decided to disguise herself as an ailing Southern gentleman traveling to Philadelphia for medical care. Her husband, William Craft, whose skin was dark, would pretend to be the "master's" doting slave. Together they would travel one thousand miles to freedom.

On December 21, 1848, they obtained passes to travel to the next town for Christmas, but their real destination was the North. They bought train tickets to Savannah, Georgia. From there, in their disguises, they traveled by train and steamboat up the coasts of South Carolina, North Carolina, Virginia, Washington, D.C., and Maryland. By Christmas Day, they had arrived in Philadelphia, a northern city. After spending three weeks with a Quaker farmer and his family, the Crafts traveled to Boston, where they found a home. William worked as a cabinetmaker, and Ellen worked as a seamstress. They lived with Lewis Hayden, a free black, whose boardinghouse often served as a safe house for fugitive slaves on the Underground Railroad. The Crafts became members of Theodore Parker's congregation.

In September 1850, the U.S. Congress passed the Fugitive Slave Law. The law not only provided for the return of fugitive slaves to their masters in the South, but also required private citizens in the North to assist in their capture. Abolitionists in Boston immediately began organizing resistance to the law. Theodore Parker was one of the founders of a Vigilance Committee designed to protect "the colored inhabitants of Boston from any invasion of their rights." The Boston Committee for Safety and Vigilance included blacks as well as whites. Lewis Hayden and William Craft were members.

On October 20, 1850, two agents arrived in Boston, sent by the Crafts' former owners to catch the fugitives. The agents took for granted that Boston officials would assist them, but in this they were disappointed. Vigilance Committee members protected the Crafts and relentlessly harassed the two slave-catchers. The coordinated actions of the abolitionist community and African Americans throughout the city thwarted the agents at every turn. The slave-catchers stayed in Boston for more than a month, trying to waylay the Crafts, but in the end, they had to return to Georgia empty-handed. The Crafts hurriedly went overseas to England, where they would be safe.

Theodore Parker wrote an angry letter to President Fillmore, telling him the story of the Craft escape and challenging him to enforce his monstrous law. "Suppose I had taken the woman to my own house, and sheltered her there till the storm had passed by: should you think I did a thing worthy of fine and imprisonment?" he asked. He made it clear that he would obey the laws of God, even if it meant breaking the laws of men.

Strange to say, Millard Fillmore, the president who had signed the Fugitive Slave Law, was also a Unitarian who hated slavery. How could his beliefs concerning the law be so different from Parker's?

"God knows I detest slavery," he wrote to Daniel Webster, his secretary of state, "but . . . we must endure it and give it such protection as is guaranteed by the Constitution till we can get rid of it without destroying the last hope of free government in the world."

President Fillmore had sworn to uphold the Constitution of the United States, and the Constitution allowed rights to slaveholders. He had promised to abide by the decisions of Congress, and they had passed a Fugitive Slave Law. He threw the weight of his influence into enforcing the Fugitive Slave Law because he believed it was the only way to keep the Union together, and he believed that safeguarding the Union was his sworn duty as president.

Those who supported the Fugitive Slave Law often stated that the purpose of government was to protect property. They argued that, since slaves were property, no one, including the slaves themselves, had any right to deprive the slaveholder of rightful ownership. A runaway slave was nothing more than a thief, in this view. They also fooled themselves into believing all sorts of falsehoods about the natural inferiority of black people. Many even convinced themselves that black people were happier in slavery than they would be if left to fend for themselves in the world.

Theodore Parker was incensed. How could the United States have strayed so far from the Revolutionary ideals of its founders? His own grandfather, Captain John Parker, had fought in Lexington, Massachusetts, in one of the very first skirmishes of the Revolutionary War. In those days, Americans had not been afraid to stand up for liberty, though it meant breaking the unjust laws imposed on them by their government in Britain. Now, this very country, founded on a principle of liberty and justice for all, was enforcing laws designed specifically to deny liberty and justice.

"There hangs in my study . . . the gun my grandfather fought with at the battle of Lexington . . . and also the musket he captured from a British soldier on that day," Parker wrote in his letter to President Fillmore. "If I would not peril my property, my liberty, nay my life to keep my parishioners out of slavery, then I should throw away these trophies, and should think I was the son of some coward and not a brave man's child."

Many other abolitionists were against using violence, but after the passage of the Fugitive Slave Law, Parker did not agree with them. He often used the proud history of the Revolution as a way of bringing people to his point of view. He also saw that over the years, there had been a practice of erasing the memory of black participation in the Revolution, and he was dedicated to reminding his fellow Americans of the historic role blacks had played.

Conflict between the northern and southern states was reaching a boiling point. Theodore Parker believed that the North must stand up against a government dominated by the interests of the Southern slaveholders. He hadn't wanted to put the abolition of slavery into the center of his life and ministry, but he felt he had no choice. Millard Fillmore hadn't wanted to support the institution of slavery, but he also felt he had no choice. He did not want his country to be divided in two.

In the end, Fillmore's signing of the Fugitive Slave Law probably did keep the country together for another ten years. And in the end, that law probably strengthened the resolve of people in the North, making it possible for them to win the Civil War. Up to that point, it was easy for Northerners to see slavery as none of their business. Whether they hated slavery or not, few Northerners considered themselves personally responsible until they were forced to participate in the capture of fugitives and to witness the kidnapping of innocent free blacks by slave-catchers.

Until the time of the Fugitive Slave Law, abolitionists had been very unpopular, even in Massachusetts. Now Theodore Parker, who had been despised by many for his radical views, suddenly became enormously popular. Every week, his sermons and speeches were heard by thousands of people and read by many more. One person who read everything by Theodore Parker that he could get his hands on was William Herndon of Illinois, Abraham Lincoln's law partner. Herndon often passed along Parker's writings to Lincoln, who expressed his admiration for them. In one sermon, Herndon had underlined the following words that he thought would interest Lincoln: "Democracy is direct self-government, over all the people, for all the people, by all the people."

Ten years later, Abraham Lincoln became the president of the United States, and the Civil War began. By then, Theodore Parker had died. He did not live to see the abolition of slavery in the United States. Yet he had helped to lay the groundwork by convincing many people that they must not blindly follow unjust laws. His words had the power to persuade many people to join the fight to end slavery.

Quotations for Discussion

One of the hazards William and Ellen Craft faced in their journey north was the possibility that Ellen's inability to read and write would be exposed. The Southern gentleman she pretended to be would certainly have been literate—but as a slave, she had been forbidden to learn. Soon after their escape, the Crafts began lessons in reading and writing; and after they reached the safety of England (December 1850), they acquired a good education. By 1852, they were able to write letters to their friends in the United States, telling about their comfortable life in England and announcing the birth of their first child. Meanwhile, their old enemies in the South continued to harass them. A preposterous rumor began circulating in proslavery newspapers, alleging that Ellen had made a deal with a white Southerner visiting London—that she had volunteered to return to slavery if he would take her back to Georgia. When she heard the rumor, Ellen wrote a letter in response, which appeared in a British antislavery newspaper. She ended with these words:

> I never had the slightest inclination of returning to bondage; and God forbid that I should be so false to liberty as to prefer slavery in its stead. In fact, since my escape from slavery, I have got on much better in every respect than I could have possibly anticipated. Though, had it been to the contrary, my feelings in regard to this would have been just the same, for I had much rather starve in England, a free woman, than be a slave for the best man that ever breathed upon the American continent.
>
> Yours very truly,
Ellen Craft

Discussion: The fact that people believed the rumor about Ellen Craft's willingness to return to slavery is an example of how people in a dominant social position assume the right to name the experience, motives, needs, and wishes of those who are oppressed. In what ways does a similar process unfold in today's world?

In 1860, William and Ellen Craft coauthored a book about their lives in slavery and the details of their daring escape. In the preface to *Running a Thousand Miles for Freedom,* William Craft wrote,

> Having heard while in Slavery that "God made of one blood all nations of men," and also that the American Declaration of Independence says, that "We hold these truths to be self-evident, that all men are created equal; that they are endowed by their Creator with certain inalienable rights; that among these, are life, liberty, and the pursuit of happiness;" we could not understand by what right we were held as "chattels." Therefore, we felt perfectly justified in undertaking the dangerous and exciting task of "running a thousand miles" in order to obtain those rights which are so vividly set forth in the Declaration.

He also wrote about his life as a slave,

> My old master had the reputation of being a very humane and Christian man, but he thought nothing of selling my poor old father, and dear aged mother, at separate times, to different persons, to be dragged off never to behold each other again, till summoned to appear before the great tribunal of heaven. But, oh! what a happy meeting it will be on that day for those faithful souls. I say a happy meeting, because I never saw persons more devoted to the service of God than they. But how will the case stand with those reckless traffickers in human flesh and blood, who plunged the poisonous dagger of separation into those loving hearts which God had for so many years closely joined together—nay, sealed as it were with his own hands for the eternal courts of heaven? It is not for me to say what will become of those heartless tyrants. I must leave them in the hands of an all-wise and just God, who will, in his own good time, and in his own way, avenge the wrongs of his oppressed people.

My old master also sold a dear brother and a sister, in the same manner as he did my father and mother. The reason he assigned for disposing of my parents, as well as of several other aged slaves, was, that "they were getting old, and would soon become valueless in the market, and therefore he intended to sell off all the old stock, and buy in a young lot." A most disgraceful conclusion for a man to come to, who made such great professions of religion! This shameful conduct gave me a thorough hatred, not for true Christianity, but for slave-holding piety.

Discussion: Craft points out that his master—and indeed all participants in the slave-holding society—did not live up to their own religious and social ideals. In what ways are we as a nation still striving to live up to our founding ideals? How are you as a Unitarian Universalist still striving to live up to your religious values and ideals?

6

Ellen and William Craft made a powerful impression on white audiences when they appeared before antislavery audiences after their escape. Samuel May, a Unitarian minister and the general agent of the Massachusetts Anti-Slavery Society, explains one important reason for their popularity in a letter to an English friend:

Ellen Craft, the young wife, is a woman who may well be called beautiful. She has no trace of African blood discernible in her features—eyes, cheeks, nose or hair, but the whole is that of a Southern-born white woman. To think of such a woman being held as a piece of property, subject to be traded off to the highest bidder (while it is in reality no worse or wickeder than when done to the blackest woman that ever was) does yet stir a community brought up in prejudice against color a thousand times more deeply than could be effected in different circumstances.

Discussion: How does this passage reveal the racial prejudice even of those who worked for the abolition of slavery? How do Samuel May's observations about the difference that lighter or darker skin color makes in arousing sympathy ring true in our own world?

Connecting with Our Lives

In Our Faith Communities

The disagreement between President Fillmore and the abolitionists is a reminder that both sides of an important debate are usually standing on what they believe to be the high moral ground. People rarely defend what they believe to be wrong, although some may fool themselves into believing that something is right simply because it promotes their own comfort. President Fillmore was not the only Unitarian to believe that compromise with the South was the best course. Many believed that chattel slavery would eventually die a natural death because industrialization would make slave labor impractical. Keeping the Union together and avoiding civil war seemed more important to them than accelerating slavery's demise. But others watched as the slave states maneuvered to ensure that chattel slavery would become legal across the entire continent, and they were outraged both by the immorality of slavery and by the base political tactics used to defend and promote it.

Convene a panel or hold a conversation in your community or congregation in which you delve deeply into the philosophical, legal, and political questions surrounding property rights as they pertain to a political or social issue of importance that involves attitudes toward property. Invite participants to address the attitudes Americans hold today concerning property rights and whether there are still some moral issues involving these rights that people disagree about. Discuss how we weigh the pros and cons when moral concerns come up against people's property rights, jobs, or personal freedoms. Encourage participants to think about whether they believe in absolutes in this area, or whether morality depends on the situation.

At Home
Everyone has prejudices of some kind. Theodore Parker, though a staunch abolitionist, was convinced that the Anglo-Saxon "race" was superior to all others. In his autobiography *Dreams from My Father*, President Barack Obama tells about discovering that his white grandmother had a deep-seated discomfort about encountering African American men on the street, despite her love for her African American grandson. Even when your rational mind accepts and believes in the equal worth of every person, do your emotions sometimes lead you in a different direction? Do you ever feel uneasy or distrustful when encountering individuals whose ethnicity or skin color is clearly very different from your own? Talk with friends or family members or write about your comfort and discomfort with people you perceive to be different from yourself. How might you begin to acknowledge and react to emotional responses which are at odds with your values and beliefs?

Find Out More

Carton, Evan. *Patriotic Treason: John Brown and the Soul of America*. New York: Free Press, 2006.

Craft, William and Ellen. *Running a Thousand Miles for Freedom; or, the Escape of William and Ellen Craft from Slavery*. London: Tweedie, 1860 (reprinted in 1969). It can be read online at the Project Gutenberg.

Fradin, Judith Bloom, and Dennis Brindell Fradin. *5,000 Miles to Freedom: Ellen and William Craft's Flight from Slavery*. Washington, D.C.: National Geographic, 2006.

Grodzins, Dean. *American Heretic: Theodore Parker and Transcendentalism*, Chapel Hill: University of North Carolina Press, 2002.

———. "Theodore Parker." *Dictionary of Unitarian and Universalist Biography*, published online by the Unitarian Universalist Historical Society at www25.uua.org/uuhs.

Herz, Walter. "Millard Fillmore." *Dictionary of Unitarian and Universalist Biography*, published online by the Unitarian Universalist Historical Society at www25.uua.org/uuhs.

Parker, Theodore. *Autobiography, Poems, Prayers.* Centenary ed. Boston: American Unitarian Association, 1911. It can be read online at Internet Archive.

Petrulionis, Sandra Harbert. *To Set This World Right: The Antislavery Movement in Thoreau's Concord.* Ithaca: Cornell University Press, 2006.

Sterling, Dorothy. *Black Foremothers: Three Lives.* Old Westbury, NY: Feminist Press, 1989.

Robert Gould Shaw and the Fifty-fourth Massachusetts Regiment

Robert Gould Shaw (1837–1863) was the son of Sarah and Francis (Frank) Shaw, two radical Unitarians who were among the first to embrace Transcendentalism, feminism, and abolitionism. The Shaws attended Emerson's lectures, and became good friends with Margaret Fuller. Through the Transcendentalists, they met other radicals and freethinkers, such as Lydia Maria Child, who soon became one of their closest friends and was instrumental in drawing them into the antislavery cause. Because the Shaws belonged to the wealthy Boston merchant class, a group generally hostile to abolition and other reforms, they seemed unlikely recruits. The principles of abolitionism made Frank Shaw so uncomfortable with his position as a businessman that, in February 1840, he bought land in West Roxbury and left his father's firm to pursue a life dedicated to scholarship and reform.

Growing up in rural West Roxbury, the young Robert Gould Shaw attended the experimental Brook Farm Institute and went to Sunday school at Theodore Parker's church. His father was a frequent visitor to Brook Farm and gave it his financial support. From the time he was thirteen years old, however, Robert attended traditional schools. His family moved to Staten Island, New York, and then to Europe. Although his parents impressed upon him that it was "man's paramount duty" to serve the human race, Robert showed little inclination to follow in their footsteps as a reformer—until he took on the awesome responsibility of commanding one of the first regiments of black troops. He accepted the challenge reluctantly but soon believed in it with all his heart.

In 1863, the Civil War was raging in the United States. It had begun more than two years earlier when some Southern states had declared that they were separating from the Union to form a separate nation called the Confederacy. Soldiers from the Confederacy were fighting to protect the Southern way of life, which depended on slave labor. Union soldiers were fighting to keep the United States together as one country. For some of them, the fight was also about abolishing slavery.

Governor John Andrew of Massachusetts was a man who cared very much about ending slavery. He also wanted to give free blacks a chance to serve in the military. For two hundred years, African Americans had been the victims of laws and practices designed to keep them servile and dependent. Few African American men had had the opportunity to demonstrate the truth of who they were. As a result, many white people believed that blacks were, by nature, less capable than whites. Many thought that African Americans would not have the courage or the discipline to be good soldiers. But Governor Andrew disagreed. He believed that black soldiers, fighting for their country, would provide a turning point in the struggle for human rights.

Governor Andrew had asked the federal government for permission to raise a regiment of free blacks to fight alongside the white regiments of the Union army. Now, more than two years into the war, he was granted permission. The Fifty-fourth Massachusetts Regiment would be the first to give free blacks from the North an opportunity to prove their worth as soldiers.

Governor Andrew knew that this experiment must not fail. The commanders of the regiment were to be experienced white officers, and Governor Andrew knew who he wanted as colonel. He chose a young captain from the Union army named Robert Gould Shaw.

Robert Shaw had been serving his country bravely since the beginning of the war. He was a well-respected young man from a wealthy family, who was committed to the Union cause. More important, he was the son of staunch abolitionists, who were passionate about the success of the project. Governor Andrew needed a commander with a strong commitment to African American rights.

At first, Shaw refused the offer. He was loyal to his own regiment and did not want to leave his comrades. Even though he had long believed that blacks should be allowed to join the Union army, he also shared some of the doubts and prejudices of many Americans. He feared that an all-black regiment would not be capable of success on the battlefield, and he feared that he was not the right person to lead them.

But after a few days, Shaw changed his mind and accepted the position after all. He could not turn his back on this cause. Even though he would have liked to stay right where he was with his familiar companions and routines, he bravely accepted the lonely, untraveled path instead.

Shaw was only twenty-five years old when he left his comrades to become the colonel of the Fifty-fourth. He had never commanded an entire regiment before. The regiment, of course, did not yet exist when he accepted the job. The first step was recruiting a thousand African American men. The next step was training them to be soldiers.

Although Robert Shaw's family was solidly behind the effort and enormously proud of the part he was playing, Shaw knew that most people would be less enthusiastic. He knew that he might be ridiculed and taunted for leading an all-black regiment. He knew that many people thought him a fool for doing it.

As Shaw began to drill the new recruits, he was exceedingly strict with them and harsh in his discipline. But as he got to know the men, his anxiety about failure faded. He soon realized that these men were among the ablest, most disciplined, and most committed soldiers anyone could have the privilege of commanding. His trust and respect grew stronger each day. Curious onlookers began coming to watch the Fifty-fourth Infantry as they marched and drilled, and soon the respect of the public grew too.

The day the Fifty-fourth Massachusetts Infantry left for the battlefield was one of the most triumphant moments of Robert Shaw's life. He rode on horseback at the head of a glorious parade through the streets of Boston. Thousands of citizens cheered and applauded as the proud ranks of blue-uniformed African American soldiers marched past.

But once Shaw and his men reached the South, many obstacles lay in their road. At first, the regiment received no important assignments, and even worse, Shaw discovered that his men were to be paid less than white soldiers. He sent letters of protest, and he encouraged his men to refuse their pay altogether until equality in pay was granted.

Then, when Shaw's regiment finally went out on a raid, they were led by a commander named Montgomery, who had a reputation for being unnecessarily destructive. They went to the beautiful town of Darien, Georgia, where they found no soldiers and no resistance. Nevertheless, Montgomery ordered his men to loot the buildings, taking whatever they wanted, and burn the town down.

Shaw was outraged. When he had first joined the army, one of his duties had been to arrest runaway slaves and return them to their owners. He had hated doing it, but he had followed orders anyway. Now, he stood firmly against injustice. He refused to participate in burning the town. Even so, his regiment was associated with the destruction of Darien because they had participated in the looting. Shaw never got over the shame he felt. He worried that the reputation of his black troops would forever be tarnished, and he worked even harder to make sure his regiment would get a chance to fight alongside whites in a battle that would bring them honor.

When the opportunity came, Shaw seized upon it. He accepted orders to lead an assault against a strong fortification known as Fort Wagner. In the days before the attack, Shaw and his troops had been exposed to soaking rains and deprived of sleep and food, but when the time came, they bravely rushed toward the earthworks that protected the fort. Colonel Shaw led his men up the steep embankment as gunfire rained down upon them. When he reached the top, he was shot, and his body fell into the enemy fort.

After the battle was over, the Confederates denied Shaw's body the honorable burial usually accorded to officers. They threw his body into a mass grave along with many of his men. They thought the act was an insult, but Robert Shaw's father turned the situation into one of glory. He let it be known that his son would have felt greatly honored to lie on the field of battle along with his men.

The story of Robert Gould Shaw's courage and commitment made him a national hero. The competence and valor of his men brought them honor and forever changed the country's reluctance to recruit black soldiers. The men of the Fifty-fourth Regiment did not win the battle at Fort Wagner, and many of them died there. But those who survived won their right to equal pay eighteen months after Shaw had led them in protest. They became the model for many successful regiments of black soldiers. When the Civil War finally ended in victory for the Union, President Lincoln believed that the black regiments had turned the tide. Robert Gould Shaw's noble sacrifice for his country and for the rights of African Americans is still remembered as a shining example of heroism for a just cause.

Quotations for Discussion

When Governor Andrew offered the command of the Fifty-fourth Massachusetts Regiment to Robert Gould Shaw, his father delivered the governor's letter in person. Robert also received a letter from his mother Sarah, in which she praised the governor's offer, and went on to say,

> Well! I feel as if God had called you up to a holy work. You helped him at a crisis when the most important question is to be solved that has been asked since the world began. I know the task is arduous . . . but it is God's work.

After Robert's refusal, she wrote a letter to Governor Andrew, saying, in part:

I just received a telegram from Mr. Shaw saying, "Rob declines. I think rightly." This decision has caused me the bitterest disappointment I have ever experienced. . . . It would have been the proudest moment of my life and I could have died satisfied that I had not lived in vain. This being the truth, you will believe that I have shed bitter tears over his refusal.

Two days later, Robert Shaw decided to accept the command after all.

Discussion: In what ways have your family, your friends, or a community of which you are a part influenced you to take up a task which you were reluctant to undertake? Did duty or responsibility play a role in your decision? Respect or friendship? What other factors played into your decision?

Many prominent blacks spoke out against enlistment. They were angry that there would be no black officers in the regiment and that blacks, who were not allowed to vote or hold office in most northern states, should be asked to fight. However, one of the most ardent recruiters for the Massachusetts Fifty-fourth was Frederick Douglass, the great orator and writer who had been born a slave and escaped to freedom. His own sons Lewis and Charles enlisted. Quoting the English poet Lord Byron, Douglass urged black men to join:

> "Who would be free themselves must strike the first blow."
> . . . I urge you to fly to arms and smite to death the power that would bury the Government and your liberty in the same hopeless grave. This is your golden opportunity.

Discussion: When, if ever, is it morally and strategically right to take up arms in response to injustice or tyranny?

Jefferson Davis, the president of the Confederate States, issued an order on December 24, 1862, saying that black soldiers were not to be treated as prisoners of war. Instead, the laws governing servile insurrection were to be applied. The orders also stipulated that captured black soldiers could be enslaved. Francis George Shaw, Robert's father, sent the following letter to Abraham Lincoln less than two weeks after his son's death, urging protection for black soldiers and their officers:

> New York 31 July 1863.
>
> Sir:
>
> My only son, Colonel Robert G. Shaw, of the Fifty fourth Regiment Massachusetts Volunteers, (colored troops) was killed on the parapet of Fort Wagner, in South Carolina, & now lies buried in its ditch, among his brave & devoted followers—
> I feel that I have the right, in his name, to entreat you that immediate measures be taken to extend the protection of the United States over his surviving officers & men, some of whom are now prisoners, & over all others belonging to the colored Regiments in the Service, when they fall into the hands of the enemy— And this, not only as an act of humanity, but as required by justice & sound policy—
> Our colored soldiers have proved their valor & devotion in the field; they deserve that their rights & the responsibilities of the Government towards them shall be proclaimed to the world & shall be maintained against all enemies—
> If our son's services & death shall contribute in any degree towards securing to our colored troops that equal justice which is the holy right of every loyal defender of our beloved Country, we shall esteem our great loss a blessing—
>
> > I am, Sir,
> > with great esteem & respect,
> > Frans Geo. Shaw

Discussion: Why is it still important to make meaning of the sacrifice of those who fight for that which we deem worthy and important? What are some ways in which we honor their memory?

Connecting with Our Lives

In Our Faith Communities
With your youth group, social action committee, or other small group, have a conversation about the use of military force in defense of values or people. Discuss the differences of opinion and approaches present in your own congregation. Encourage participants to consider their points of agreement. Invite them to consider what actions your congregation is willing to take in support of those in the military or of their families.

At Home
What is the value of heroic legends such as this one? Obtain and watch the 1989 Hollywood movie *Glory,* based on the story of Robert Gould Shaw and the Massachusetts Fifty-fourth. Does the film seem true to history? Does it give you a sense of pride in your beliefs or your country? What questions does it make you ask about right and wrong, war and peace?

Find Out More

Blatt, Martin Henry, Thomas J. Brown, and Donald Yacovone, eds. *Hope & Glory: Essays on the Legacy of the 54th Massachusetts Regiment.* Amherst: University of Massachusetts Press, 2001.

Duncan, Russell. *Where Death and Glory Meet: Colonel Shaw and the 54th Massachusetts Infantry.* Athens: The University of Georgia Press, 1999.

"The Fifty-fourth Massachusetts Infantry" on the United States Civil War site at www.us-civilwar.com.

Foote, Lorien. *Seeking the One Great Remedy: Francis George Shaw and Nineteenth Century Reform.* Athens: Ohio University Press, 2003.

Shaw, Francis George, to Abraham Lincoln, Friday, July 31, 1863, in the Abraham Lincoln Papers at the Library of Congress website at www.loc.gov.

Shaw, Robert Gould. *Blue-Eyed Child of Fortune: The Civil War Letters of Colonel Robert Gould Shaw,* ed. Russell Duncan. Athens: The University of Georgia Press, 1992.

Women's Rights

Lucy Stone and Henry Blackwell Redefine Marriage

Although she grew up on a humble farm, without wealth or educational advantages, Lucy Stone (1818–1893) graduated with honors from Oberlin College in Ohio in 1847, the first woman from Massachusetts to earn a college degree. She had not been able to begin college until she was twenty-five years old because, in the words of her daughter Alice Stone Blackwell, "At the low wages then paid to women, it took Lucy nine years to save up money enough to enter college. There was no difficulty as to the choice of an alma mater. There was only one college that admitted women."

Lucy Stone had a strong interest in debate and public speaking, yet even at Oberlin, training in these skills was reserved for men only. She and her best friend Antoinette Brown, who later became the first ordained female minister in the United States, began their own debating society off campus. Despite a tradition prohibiting public speaking by women before mixed audiences, Stone soon became known as a powerful orator. She decided on a career as a public lecturer at a time when only a small handful of women had dared to lecture in public at all, and they were widely reviled for doing so.

For many years, Lucy Stone had been a loyal supporter of William Lloyd Garrison's antislavery newspaper the Liberator, *and after she graduated from college, the Anti-Slavery Society offered her a job in Massachusetts as an "agent." An agent was a speaker but was also responsible for booking halls, getting out the publicity, planning transportation, and attending to all the organizational details necessary for a successful speaking engagement. Her speeches were soon attracting large* audiences. *Officials of the Anti-Slavery Society were pleased with her popularity, but they were troubled when she included women's rights messages in her antislavery speeches. The cause of women's rights was even more unpopular than abolition, and many abolitionists feared that any hint of feminism would alienate powerful groups whose support they needed. For Stone, the women's rights issue was paramount. She decided to strike out on her own as a women's rights lecturer. The Anti-Slavery Society reached a compromise with her: They would pay her to deliver antislavery lectures on weekends, and she would schedule and finance her own women's rights lectures on weekdays.*

During Stone's childhood, the rights of women in the United States had sunk to a very low point. White males had gained near total control over their wives' property and earnings, as well as sole custody of their children. To avoid submitting to the political and economic injustices of the marriage laws, Stone had vowed never to become a wife.

At seven o'clock in the morning on May 1, 1855, a small group of family and friends gathered in a Massachusetts farmhouse for the wedding of Lucy Stone and Henry Blackwell. The groom opened the ceremony by reading a marriage protest that he and the bride had both signed. It stated that they had chosen to marry each other despite the unjust laws that gave a husband ownership of his wife and all her property. They pledged to live not by the existing marriage laws but in "an equal and permanent partnership."

After the protest, the bride and groom said their vows. They vowed to love and honor each other—but left out the usual bride's vow to obey. Then the minister—a well-known abolitionist and reformer named Thomas Wentworth Higginson—joined their hands and pronounced them husband and wife. After a quick celebratory breakfast, the newlyweds hurried off to catch an 8:20 train. In a letter to his mother, Higginson said it was "the most beautiful bridal I ever attended." He published the couple's marriage protest in the *Worcester Spy*, and it was soon picked up by newspapers nationwide.

What made the wedding especially newsworthy was Lucy Stone's fame. Although she advocated the unpopular causes of abolition and women's rights, she was one of the most popular speakers on the lecture circuit. By the time of her marriage, Lucy Stone had lectured in seventeen states, the District of Columbia, and Canada. She was renowned for her beautiful voice and her sweet temperament. In those years, rowdies often disrupted antislavery and women's rights lectures, making it impossible for any speaker, male or female, to be heard. Lucy Stone had a remarkable ability to quiet even the rowdiest crowds and to hold them spellbound for the duration of her speeches.

And now, here was the surprising news that Lucy Stone, at age thirty-seven, had decided to marry. She had been dead-set against marriage for a very long time. The Bible verse that said, "Thy desire shall be to thy husband, and he shall rule over thee" had deeply upset her as a child. She knew very well that the laws of men were unfair to women, but she did not believe that God was against women. The verse must be a mistake in translation, she decided. She resolved to study Hebrew and Greek so that she could read the Bible as it was written. And she also resolved never to marry if it meant she must be ruled by a man.

Lucy managed to get the education she wanted by traveling to Oberlin College in Ohio—the only college that accepted women at that time. In 1847, she became the first woman from Massachusetts to earn a college degree. She had fought for equal opportunities and equal pay while at Oberlin, and the injustices she had faced along the way only strengthened her resolve not to marry.

Henry Blackwell knew about Stone's beliefs before he set out to court her. How could he not know? As Elizabeth Cady Stanton, another activist for women's rights, later said of Stone, "She was the first speaker who really stirred the nation's heart on the subject of women's wrongs. Young, magnetic, eloquent, her soul filled with the new idea, she drew immense audiences, and was eulogized everywhere by the press."

Lucy Stone stirred the nation's heart—yes, and also Henry's. He heard her speak in New York and was smitten. He next heard her speak at the State House in Boston and decided he must marry her. Henry Blackwell was no stranger to strong-minded women. His sister Elizabeth was the first woman in America to receive a medical degree, and he had other sisters who were equally ambitious.

But if Henry was to marry Lucy, he would first have to meet her. He asked the abolitionist William Lloyd Garrison to write a letter of introduction for him. Then he headed out to the rural Massachusetts farmhouse where Lucy was staying with her parents. He found her standing on a table, whitewashing the ceiling.

Henry stayed to supper. Then he and Lucy took a walk to the summit of a hill. As they gazed at the view, he wasted no time in getting right to the point of his visit. Lucy was nearly caught off balance by the eloquence of his proposal. But she agreed to be friends, nothing more.

Their courtship was mostly by mail, since Henry lived in Cincinnati, and Lucy was traveling the country, lecturing. Sometimes Henry traveled to where she was so that they could talk to each other in person. He made himself useful by arranging a western lecture tour for her, and he convinced her to visit him and meet his family in Ohio. For two years, he argued his case. He would never demand rights that she herself did not grant him. Marriage would strengthen her position as an advocate for the rights of married women, not weaken it.

At last, Lucy gave in. She had grown to love Henry and wished to try out this bold experiment of marriage as a partnership of equals. But she did not agree to change her name. To Lucy, when a woman lost her name, it symbolized her loss of personhood in marriage. She consulted legal experts and learned that there was no law requiring wives to change their names. She signed her name Lucy Stone (only) for the rest of her life and was the first married woman in America to keep her own name.

Soon after her marriage, Lucy received a letter from her friend Susan B. Anthony, urging her to get her husband's permission to attend a convention in New York. Lucy was surprised that Susan, a fellow worker in the woman suffrage movement, would suppose she could no longer make her own decisions. She told Anthony that she had shown the letter to Henry and asked whether she might go. "Only think of it," she wrote, "he did not give me permission but told me to ask Lucy Stone! I can't get him to govern me at all!"

Henry Blackwell had promised his wife the right to govern herself when they made their marriage protest. He had also promised to assist her in promoting the cause of women's rights, and he was faithful to his word. He was one of the few men who regularly attended the annual women's rights conventions. He also attended Republican Party conventions and tried to convince other men to adopt a woman suffrage plank. Together, he and Stone helped to found the New England Woman Suffrage Association, the Massachusetts Woman Suffrage Association, and the American Woman Suffrage Association. They founded the *Woman's Journal,* an important feminist newspaper, in 1870, and they both served as editors until 1893, when Lucy Stone died.

After her death, Henry continued his work for women's rights. The Massachusetts Woman Suffrage Association presented him an award in 1905, "In gratitude for his unswerving support of his beloved wife, Lucy Stone, in her life work, and for his fifty years of unselfish and untiring labor for the enfranchisement of women." In his response, he spoke of the assurance he had given Lucy during their courtship that, together, they could do more for women's rights than she could do alone. "If she had not believed that it might be so," he said, "she never would have married."

On her deathbed, Lucy beckoned her daughter Alice to bend near. "Make the world better," she whispered. These words expressed her own hopes when she married a man who would join her in redefining marriage as a partnership of equals. And these words were, without a doubt, the words that had guided her own work throughout her life.

Quotations for Discussion

Henry Blackwell read the following marriage protest aloud at his wedding to Lucy Stone on May 1, 1855. Rev. Thomas Wentworth Higginson published it so that other couples might follow the example:

> While acknowledging our mutual affection by publicly assuming the relationship of husband and wife, yet in justice to ourselves and a great principle, we deem it our duty to declare that this act on our part implies no sanction of, nor promise of voluntary obedience to such of the present laws of marriage, as refuse to recognize the wife as an independent, rational being, while they confer upon the husband an injurious and unnatural superiority, investing him with legal powers which no honorable man would exercise, and which no man should possess. We protest especially against the laws which give to the husband:
>
> 1. The custody of the wife's person.
> 2. The exclusive control and guardianship of their children.
> 3. The sole ownership of her personal, and use of her real estate, unless previously settled upon her or placed in the hands of trustees, as in the case of minors, lunatics, and idiots.
> 4. The absolute right to the product of her industry.
> 5. Also against laws which give to the widower so much larger and more permanent interest in the property of his deceased wife, than they give to the widow in that of the deceased husband.
> 6. Finally, against the whole system by which the legal existence of the wife is suspended during marriage, so that in most States, she neither has a legal part in the choice of her residence, nor can she make a will, nor sue or be sued in her own name, nor inherit property.

> We believe that personal independence and equal human rights can never be forfeited, except for crime; that marriage should be an equal and permanent partnership and so recognized by law; that until it is so recognized, married partners should provide against the radical injustice of present laws, by every means in their power.
>
> We believe that where domestic difficulties arise, no appeal should be made to legal tribunals under existing laws, but that all difficulties should be submitted to the equitable adjustment of arbitrators mutually chosen.
>
> Thus, reverencing law, we enter our protest against rules and customs which are unworthy of the name since they violate justice, the essence of law.

Discussion: Stone and Blackwell chose to participate in the institution of marriage while still protesting the laws of their time, using their influence to help change the law. Describe a time in your life when you chose to participate in an unjust system while at the same time working to change it.

At the time Henry Blackwell began courting Lucy Stone, she was wearing the "short dress"—a dress that came just below the knees, with trousers under it—commonly called the "Bloomer." She and other women's rights advocates wore this comfortable and practical style from about 1851 to 1853, but eventually gave it up because of the negative attention it drew. In one of Henry's earliest letters to Lucy (July 2, 1853), he wrote,

> Do you know I quite envy you your position as lecturer, engaged in the advocacy of great though unpopular ideas. With all its privations & sacrifices, it is an intellectual life & one identified with principles & elevated by them. Above all, it is a useful one, preparing the way for the *good time* in which you have so devout & beautiful a faith. The very *isolation*,

which your opinions, your occupation, above all your dress necessarily incur, has something to me strangely attractive. In thought as in Nature there is something bracing in the air of solitude. I am myself naturally social in all my tastes and habits. I love even too well the sympathy and approbation of my fellow creatures. And therefore I love & reverence the more the motives which lead you to devote yourself to the highest Truth you can attain & *to live your own life* regardless of all the losses which consistency may entail upon you.

Discussion: Have you ever felt isolated by taking a position against an injustice? Where do you find support when your position makes you unpopular?

Lucy's mixed emotions about her unmarried state can be seen in letters she wrote to Antoinette Brown. Lucy and Antoinette (Nettie) met at Oberlin College and became fast friends. They both resolved not to marry and were steadfast in their resolve until the mid-1850s. They became sisters-in-law in 1856 when Antoinette married Samuel Blackwell, Henry's brother. But in the summer of 1849, Lucy wrote to Antoinette,

> It seems to me that *no* man who *deserved* the *name* MAN, when he knows what a *mere thing* the law makes a married woman, would ever insult a woman by asking her to marry.

On the other hand, she confided that she found single life a "wretchedly unnatural way of living," and she hoped the two of them might bring down the laws that kept a married woman from "having any being of her own." She told Antoinette,

> I have not yet reached the place where I need no companionship as you have. It is horrid to live without the intimate companionship and gentle loving influences which are the constant attendants of a true love marriage.

Discussion: How did Lucy Stone manage to balance her personal life and her calling to do the work of justice in the world? Have you ever had to find such a balance? Are there other contemporary or historical reformers who faced similar challenges?

Connecting with Our Lives

In Our Faith Communities

Julia Ward Howe (1819–1910) was a prominent spokesperson for women's rights throughout the last third of the nineteenth century. She edited the *Woman's Journal* with Lucy Stone and Henry Blackwell from 1872 to 1879. She had not been interested in the women's rights movement until, at the urging of Thomas Wentworth Higginson, she attended a meeting for woman suffrage in Boston in 1868. According to an account written by her daughters, "She saw now for the first time the sweet face of Lucy Stone, heard the silver voice which was to be dear to her through many years." The encounter was a turning point in Howe's life and helped her cast off the restraints upon her public life that her husband had always imposed. In her *Reminiscences* (1899), she wrote,

> During the first two thirds of my life I looked to the masculine ideal of character as the only true one. I sought its inspiration, and referred my merits and demerits to its judicial verdict. In an unexpected hour a new light came to me, showing me a world of thought and of character quite beyond the limits within which I had hitherto been content to abide. The new domain now made clear to me was that of true womanhood,—woman no longer in her ancillary relation to her opposite, man, but in her direct relation to the divine plan and purpose, as a free agent, fully sharing with man every human right and every human responsibility. This discovery was like the addition of a new continent to the map of the world. . . .
>
> One of the comforts which I found in the new association was the relief which it afforded me from a sense of

isolation and eccentricity. For years past I had felt strongly impelled to lend my voice to the convictions of my heart.... I now found a sphere of action in which this mode of expression no longer appeared singular or eccentric, but simple, natural, and, under the circumstances, inevitable.

Julia Ward Howe speaks of finding a group of like-minded people as a way of finding oneself. The women's movement in Howe and Stone's time raised self-esteem and provided an escape from the isolation that was the lot of most nineteenth-century wives, and the sense of being peculiar and unacceptable that was the lot of most independent-minded, intellectual women.

In our own time, many seek connections within their Unitarian Universalist congregation rather than going it alone in the work of bringing more love and justice into the world. Invite congregational leaders and small groups to reflect on how your congregation nurtures connections among parishioners and how your social justice ministry is strengthened by the care and compassion people experience within your faith community.

At Home
As a sister, teacher, wife, mother, and friend, Lucy Stone lived by her conviction that nothing is gained by presenting ideas or opinions with a tone of hostility or antagonism. If you want people to listen, she had found, you must not arouse their feelings of anger or resentment. One reason for her success as a public speaker was her way of giving audiences confidence that she sympathized with their position before she tried to persuade them to look at things from a different point of view. Even when she wanted people to recognize injustice and join the battle against it, she did not speak in an angry or strident way.

Lucy had taught herself these skills as a child. Once, she caught sight of her own reflection in a mirror when she was angrily chasing her sister through the house. She was horrified by what she saw, and she pledged that she would never again speak or act when she was in such an angry state. After that, she sometimes ran outside and stayed out until she had gained control of herself. In her later life, she was well-known for her calm and reasoned approach to conflict. Few suspected how difficult it had been for her to gain control of her own temper.

Talk with your family about Lucy's practices to help her control her temper. What positive results might occur if your family adopted her techniques to work out disagreements? Does her method present challenges or drawbacks? Decide together what your family's current approach is to anger and conflict. Are there things you would like to change? Can you develop some approaches you might try that would help everyone cool off before anger gets in the way of a reasonable and fair discussion?

Find Out More

Blackwell, Alice Stone. *Lucy Stone: Pioneer of Woman's Rights.* Boston: Little, Brown, 1930. Reprinted by Grand River Books, Detroit, 1971.

Hanaford, Phebe A. *Daughters of America.* Augusta, ME: True and Co., 1882. It can be read online at Google Books.

Kerr, Andrea Moore. *Lucy Stone: Speaking Out for Equality.* New Brunswick, NJ: Rutgers University Press, 1992.

Million, Joelle. *Woman's Voice, Woman's Place: Lucy Stone and the Birth of the Woman's Rights Movement.* Westport, CT: Praeger Publishers, 2003.

Stone, Lucy. *Loving Warriors: Selected Letters of Lucy Stone and Henry B. Blackwell, 1853–1893*, ed. and introd. Leslie Wheeler. New York: Dial Press, 1981.

Susan B. Anthony's Challenges and Devotion

Susan B. Anthony (1820–1906) was brought up in a Quaker family that joined the Unitarian Church in Rochester, New York, following a split among Quakers over the issue of slavery. Throughout her life, Anthony maintained sympathies with Quakerism, but she regularly attended the Unitarian Church for her "Sunday uplifts." She did not become interested in the women's rights movement until 1850, when she read a speech that Lucy Stone had delivered at the first National Women's Rights Convention in Worcester, Massachusetts. Horace Greeley had published the proceedings of the convention in his New York Tribune—and by good fortune, Anthony soon had the chance to meet both Horace Greeley and Lucy Stone at the home of Elizabeth Cady Stanton in Seneca Falls, New York. Stanton, a young wife and mother, was becoming a well-known activist for women's rights. She and Lucretia Mott had organized the first Woman's Rights Conventions in upstate New York in 1848. Their Declaration of Sentiments, signed by sixty-eight women and thirty-two men, had set the agenda for the women's rights movement.

Anthony and Stanton formed a working partnership and a close friendship in the early 1850s that lasted for the rest of their lives. In the early years, the brilliant Mrs. Stanton was tied down by an ever-expanding houseful of children. She wrote speeches for Anthony and helped formulate strategies, while Anthony did most of the legwork—gathering information, attending meetings, distributing literature, and circulating petitions.

The energetic and hard-working Anthony became known to a wider circle of activists when she attended the third annual Woman's

Rights Convention in 1852. Lucy Stone organized and managed the first seven national conventions, but when she became a mother in 1857, she passed the responsibility for annual conventions on to Anthony, who proved to be a very able successor. Over the next fifty years, Susan B. Anthony became the best-known leader in the movement.

Sadly, a rift tore the women's rights movement apart in 1869, with Susan B. Anthony and Elizabeth Cady Stanton on one side, and Lucy Stone, Antoinette Brown Blackwell, and Julia Ward Howe on the other. A discussion of the issues that kept the two sides apart for more than twenty years is beyond the scope of this story. Yet the disagreement described here, which led to the split, serves to illustrate the difficulties faced by reformers everywhere. It is difficult to know how to handle a disappointing setback. It is hard to figure out which compromises and alliances will advance the cause. In this story, Susan B. Anthony stands firm for woman suffrage even when it means losing some of her closest friends and allies.

Susan B. Anthony was a teacher in Canajoharie, New York, when she delivered her first public speech. As the presiding officer of the local Daughters of Temperance, she urged women to eliminate alcohol consumption, not just within their own families but throughout society. Her speech ended with a stirring call to action: "Ladies! There is no Neutral position for us to assume. . . . If we say we love the Cause, and then sit down at our ease, surely does our action speak the lie." No words could better describe Susan B. Anthony's approach to life. Once she had committed herself to a cause, she gave it her all. She was not one to sit down at her ease.

Anthony quit her teaching job soon after delivering that speech and returned to her parents' farm in Rochester, New York. She had decided to dedicate her life to social reform. While she had been away, her parents and sister had attended a women's rights convention. They had signed a declaration that said women should have the right to vote. Despite their enthusiasm, Susan thought little of it. She was far more interested in the antislavery meetings that took place in her parents' house every Sunday, and she was still campaigning for temperance. Only gradually did she begin to commit herself to the cause of women's rights.

An important moment came in 1851, when Susan B. Anthony met Elizabeth Cady Stanton, the young wife and mother who had drafted the Declaration of Sentiments that Anthony's parents and sister had signed. Stanton and Anthony hit it off at once, beginning one of the most famous friendships in the history of reform. Anthony was a superb and tireless organizer, and Stanton an excellent writer, bursting with ideas.

The two women first worked as a team the following year. At a statewide temperance convention, Anthony stood to speak. The chairman silenced her, saying, "The sisters were not invited . . . to speak but to listen and learn." Anthony stalked out of the hall and resolved to form a statewide temperance society run by women. She asked Stanton to be its first president.

When the five hundred members of the new Woman's State Temperance Society met for the first time, Stanton proposed a program that went far beyond eliminating liquor. She believed that women needed new divorce laws to protect themselves and their children from alcoholic husbands. She also believed women needed the right to vote if they hoped to change the laws. Most of the delegates were shocked by her radical ideas. The next time the Society met, the conservative majority voted Stanton out and refused to discuss either woman suffrage or divorce. Susan B. Anthony had worked hard to build the organization, but she immediately resigned in protest. Stanton told her not to feel disappointed. "We have other and bigger fish to fry," she said. And they did.

Susan B. Anthony began attending woman's rights conventions. Two leaders in the movement, Lucy Stone and Antoinette Brown, mentored her and became her close friends. She began giving lectures, and she campaigned with Elizabeth Stanton to reform New York's laws concerning married women's property rights. She was becoming a leader in the cause.

During this time, the nation was being torn apart by the controversy over slavery. In 1856, Anthony accepted a job with the American Anti-Slavery Society. She maintained her firm commitment to women's rights, but she understood that abolition was the first priority for most reformers during the period of national unrest and civil war. Little did she imagine that the cause of women's rights would encounter an even greater setback when the war was over.

A Constitutional amendment was required to secure full citizenship for the freed slaves after the United States Civil War. Congress drafted the Fourteenth Amendment, which, for the first time, defined voters as *male* citizens. The women who had been working tirelessly for universal suffrage were aghast. They formed an American Equal Rights Association to advocate for equal rights for *all* people, regardless of race or gender. But the Fourteenth Amendment passed as written, forcing advocates to work harder than ever to secure equal rights for women.

During the campaign for woman suffrage in 1867, a split emerged within the movement. Anthony and Stanton joined a wealthy Democrat named George Train on a speaking tour. Until then, the Republican Party had been the party of equal rights, but it seemed to be turning its back on woman suffrage. Train was a Northerner who had supported the South. He was openly racist and made many outrageously bigoted jokes and remarks during his speeches. But Anthony and Stanton were willing to work with him because he supported votes for women and was popular with audiences. Best of all, he had offered to finance a woman suffrage newspaper.

Old friends began to distance themselves. They did not want woman suffrage to be associated with Train's racism. The disagreement became even more heated when Congress passed the Fifteenth Amendment, which explicitly gave the ballot to black men but not to women. Up to that time, abolitionists such as Wendell Phillips, William Lloyd Garrison, and Frederick Douglass—members of the American Equal Rights Association—had been women's staunchest allies. But now these men declared that it was the "Negro's Hour." They did not believe the amendment would succeed if combined with woman suffrage. Giving the vote to former slaves was urgent, they argued. The Ku Klux Klan and other white supremacy organizations had initiated waves of violence throughout the nation. Blacks were publicly murdered with alarming frequency. The time had come to enfranchise African American men. Women could wait.

To Anthony, this was a stunning betrayal. These were the men who had stood by her side as long as she had been in the movement. The desertion of Frederick Douglass was perhaps the most painful. The eloquent former slave had been a pillar of support to the woman suffrage movement ever since its inception, and he was a family friend too. Just three years earlier, he had delivered a eulogy at her father's funeral.

Most of the women at the 1869 Equal Rights Convention voted with the men to support the Fifteenth Amendment, believing it would bring the nation one step closer to full equality. Anthony and Stanton strongly disagreed. They believed it was a step backwards, because it allowed uneducated black men to vote ahead of educated white women and would make the "degradation" of women "more complete." They left the meeting in anger and formed a National Woman Suffrage Association that would oppose ratification of the Fifteenth Amendment. A few months later, the suffragists who supported the amendment formed their own organization called the American Woman Suffrage Association. The women's movement was officially divided in two.

After the Fifteenth Amendment was ratified by the states, the initial reason for the rift between the two associations no longer existed. But new issues had come between them. Twenty years passed before they finally joined together in 1890.

In the meantime, the two suffrage associations worked separately for common goals, and each made important gains for women. No one was more devoted to the work than Susan B. Anthony. Her National Woman Suffrage Association met every year in Washington, D. C., and year after year, she put pressure on Congress to pass a new Constitutional amendment giving women the right to vote.

The amendment did not pass in Anthony's lifetime, but her commitment to the cause never wavered, nor did her faith. Near the end of her life, she proclaimed that, with so many true and loyal women devoted to the cause, "failure is impossible." And when the United States Constitution was finally amended to give voting rights to women, the amendment was called the Susan B. Anthony Amendment in her honor.

Quotations for Discussion

The Fourteenth Amendment to the Constitution, ratified in 1868, used the word *male* for the first time to define which citizens must not be denied the right to vote. The Fifteenth Amendment, passed in February 1869, stated that "the right of citizens of the United States to vote shall not be denied or abridged . . . on account of race, color, or previous condition of servitude." Susan B. Anthony refused to support ratification of either amendment. For her, universal suffrage was the only acceptable wording. The following excerpts are from her discussion with Frederick Douglass at the 1869 convention of the American Equal Rights Association:

> *Frederick Douglass*: I must say that I do not see how any one can pretend that there is the same urgency in giving the ballot to woman as to the negro. With us, the matter is a question of life and death, at least in fifteen States of the Union. When women, because they are women, are hunted down through the cities of New York and New Orleans; when they are dragged from their houses and hung upon lamp-posts; when their children are torn from their arms, and their brains dashed out upon the pavement; when they are objects of insult and outrage at every turn; when they are in danger of having their homes burnt down over their heads; when

their children are not allowed to enter schools; then they will have the urgency to obtain the ballot equal to our own.

A voice: Is that not all true about black women?

Douglass: Yes, yes, yes, it is true of the black woman, but not because she is a woman, but because she is black. . . .

Susan B. Anthony: If Mr. Douglass had noticed who clapped [applauded] him when he said "black men first & white women afterwards," he would have seen that they were all men. The women did not clap [applaud] him. The proof is that the men cannot understand us women. They think of us as some of the slaveholders used to think of their slaves, all love & compassion, with no malice in their hearts; but they thought "The Negro is a poor lovable creature, kind, docile, unable to take care of himself, & dependent on our compassion to keep them"; & so they consented to do it for the good of the slaves. Men . . . think that women are perfectly contented to let men earn the money & dole it out to us. We feel with Alexander Hamilton, "Give a man power over my substance & he has power over my whole being." . . .

When Mr. Douglass tells us that the cause of the black man is so perilous I tell him that wronged & outraged as they are by this hateful & mean prejudice against color, he would not today exchange his sex & color, wronged as he is, with Elizabeth Cady Stanton. . . .

What we demand is that woman shall have the ballot, for she will never get her other rights until she demands them with the ballot in her hand. It is not a question of precedence between women and black men. Neither has a claim to precedence upon an Equal Rights platform. But the business of this association is to demand for every man black or white, & for every woman, black or white, that they shall be this instant enfranchised & admitted into the body politic with equal rights & privileges.

Discussion: How do you respond to Anthony's and Douglass's differing positions when confronted with competing claims for justice and equality? How does this long-ago debate resonate in our contemporary society? What current examples can you think of in which there are still competing claims for justice, and advocates are faced with strategic choices?

African American women's rights activists Sojourner Truth and Frances Ellen Watkins Harper came down on opposite sides in the disagreement over the Fifteenth Amendment. Harper, a member of the American Equal Rights Association, chose to support the vote for black men. She was glad that at least some of the freed slaves would soon have a voice. Sojourner Truth, on the other hand, sided with Susan B. Anthony, saying,

> There is a great stir about colored men getting their rights, but not a word about the colored women; and if colored men get their rights, and not colored women theirs, you see the colored men will be masters over the women, and it will be just as bad as it was before.

Discussion: What light does this debate shed on how groups with overlapping interests and priorities work together for social justice? How do we find common ground in our work for justice even when there are differences in our strategic priorities and approaches?

The funeral of Susan B. Anthony in 1906 drew ten thousand mourners. At the funeral, Anna Howard Shaw, president of the National American Woman Suffrage Association at that time, said of her:

She knew that where freedom is, there is the center of power. In it she saw potentially all that humanity might attain when possessed by its spirit. Hence her cause, perfect equality of rights, of opportunity, of privilege for all, civil and political—was to her the bed-rock upon which all true progress must rest. Therefore *she* was nothing, her *cause* was everything. She knew no existence apart from it. In it she lived and moved and had her being. It was the first and last thought of each day.

Discussion: How did her single-minded devotion to women's rights serve both Anthony and the cause? What benefits do you see to her approach—for herself and for all women? What drawbacks were there?

On February 15, 1894 (her seventy-fourth birthday), at the annual convention of the National American Woman Suffrage Association in Washington, D.C., Susan B. Anthony said,

We shall some day be heeded, and when we shall have our amendment to the Constitution of the United States, everybody will think it was always so, just exactly as many young people believe that all the privileges, all the freedom, all the enjoyments which woman now possesses always were hers. They have no idea of how every single inch of ground that she stands upon today has been gained by the hard work of some little handful of women of the past.

Discussion: How do we honor those whose work in the cause of justice and equality continues to benefit society today? Upon whose shoulders does your own social justice work rest?

☾

Universalist Clara Barton, Civil War nurse, humanitarian, and founder of the American Red Cross, said in 1906,

> A few days ago some one said to me that every woman should stand with bared head before Susan B. Anthony. "Yes," I answered, "and every man as well." I would not retract these words. I believe that man has benefited by her work as much as woman. For ages he has been trying to carry the burden of life's responsibilities alone and when he has the efficient help of woman he will be grateful. Just now it is new and strange and men cannot comprehend what it would mean but the change is not far away. The nation is soon to have woman suffrage and it will be a glad and proud day when it comes.

Discussion: Has time proven Barton right? How have men benefited from the changes in women's status that have taken place since 1906?

Connecting with Our Lives

In Our Faith Communities

Susan B. Anthony and Elizabeth Cady Stanton were believers in the abolitionist cause, yet they used scare tactics about ignorant blacks and immigrants when arguing in favor of woman suffrage. From the beginning, Anthony argued that if men in power "are determined to extend suffrage piece by piece, then give it first to women, to the most intelligent and capable of them, at least, because in the present state of government, it is intelligence, it is morality, which is needed." Stage a debate, arguing the two sides of the 1869 disagreement about universal suffrage. Following the debate, invite small groups, your youth group, or your social action committee to explore what lessons this era in history offers for our own social justice work today. Ask how we can honor the work done by our forebears in the cause of equality while at the same time decrying behavior and words which we now find offensive.

At Home

Through her temperance work, Susan B. Anthony met Amelia Bloomer, whose newspaper *The Lily* was the first woman-owned newspaper in the United States. It was while visiting Bloomer in Seneca Falls that Anthony met Elizabeth Cady Stanton.

At the time, Stanton was experimenting with a new kind of dress. In those days, women were expected to wear large, cumbersome dresses with tight bodices and long, full skirts. Imagine having to climb the stairs in such clothing with a baby in one hand and a candle in the other. Imagine having to travel with a large trunk just to carry one dress.

In 1851, Stanton's cousin Elizabeth Smith Miller devised a new style consisting of a looser and shorter dress worn with trousers underneath. Stanton adopted the style immediately, and her friend Amelia Bloomer publicized its comfort and practicality in her newspaper. Soon many champions of women's rights, including Susan B. Anthony, adopted the short dress. Those who wore it also called it the "freedom dress," but its critics called it the "Bloomer."

Unfortunately, America was not ready for dress reform. The women who wore the Bloomer in public endured much ridicule and harassment. After a couple of years, Stanton decided to give up the dress. Anthony held on for a few more months. Once committed to a cause, she hated to abandon it. But she eventually realized that the distraction of the dress was getting in the way of the women's rights message, and she too gave it up.

Initiate a conversation with your family about what the adoption and eventual abandonment of the freedom dress teaches. To what extent can a person dress in styles outside the norm today in school, in public life, or at work? Would you dare to face ridicule and abuse for your right to be comfortable or to make a statement with your clothing? In the case of the Bloomer dress, women who privately supported dress reform were very upset when public leaders like Susan B. Anthony and Lucy Stone gave it up. They believed that leading spokespersons should continue to wear it in order to defend their right to choose for themselves what to wear. Which would you do in their situation—defend a principle by continuing to wear it, or give it up?

Find Out More

Anthony, Katharine. *Susan B. Anthony: Her Personal History and Her Era.* New York: Doubleday, 1954.

Barry, Kathleen. *Susan B. Anthony: A Biography of a Singular Feminist.* New York: New York University Press, 1988.

Lutz, Alma. *Susan B. Anthony: Rebel, Crusader, Humanitarian.* Boston: Beacon Press, 1959. It can be read online at Project Gutenberg.

Sherr, Lynn. *Failure Is Impossible: Susan B. Anthony in Her Own Words.* New York: Times Books, 1995.

Ward, Geoffrey C., and Burns, Ken. *Not for Ourselves Alone: The Story of Elizabeth Cady Stanton and Susan B. Anthony.* New York: Alfred A. Knopf, 1999.

Olympia Brown Gets the Vote

As a young girl, Olympia Brown (1835–1926) moved with her family from Vermont to a farm in Michigan. Her Universalist parents were dedicated to providing the best educational opportunities they could for their daughters as well as their sons. Olympia wanted very much to go to college, but in the 1850s, few colleges accepted women. After an unhappy year at Mount Holyoke Female Seminary in Massachusetts, she looked for other options. There were only two coeducational colleges to consider: Antioch and Oberlin, both in Ohio. She chose Antioch College over Oberlin when she heard that Lucy Stone had not been allowed to speak at her Oberlin graduation ceremony. Olympia Brown was already quite certain that her future would include public speaking.

The president of Antioch College was Horace Mann, a prominent Unitarian married to Elizabeth Peabody's sister Mary. He had transformed public education in Massachusetts before moving to Ohio. Two months before his death, Mann challenged the Antioch graduating class of 1859 with the famous words, "Be ashamed to die until you have won some victory for humanity."

Olympia Brown, who graduated from Antioch the following year, certainly lived up to his challenge. Determination, talent, and hard work gave her the strength to break through the barriers that kept women from careers in the ministry. In 1863, she became the first woman ordained as a Universalist minister. Ten years later, she married John Henry Willis, and they had two children. She was aided in maintaining both a demanding career and a family by her very supportive husband and by her mother, who joined their household and helped care for the children. Like Lucy Stone, Olympia Brown kept her own name after marriage.

An activist for women's rights even before she left the full-time ministry to devote herself to the cause, she was one of the very few from the early days of the woman suffrage movement who lived to cast a vote in a national election.

A farm wagon bumped along through the Kansas prairie under a blazing August sun. Next to the wagon's driver sat a young woman in a long black dress. She had been up since four a.m. and, after a hasty breakfast, had taken her leave. Now, as her eyes took in the great sweep of prairie that spread out around her, Olympia Brown had plenty of time to gather her thoughts. It was a long way to the next town where folks would come to hear her speak.

She had met the driver only the day before. The track they were traveling wasn't really a road at all. They made their way through the sea of tall grass, with no hint of a town or a village ahead. But after a month of similar days, Brown had faith that she would indeed reach a town where people would gather to hear her speak. She had faith that someone would provide her a meal and a place to sleep (though it might be no more than a rough mattress on the floor of a sod house). And she had faith that someone would transport her to the town where she was scheduled to speak the following day.

Olympia Brown was not a complainer. She had a job to do, and she did it with strength and conviction and enormous good will. But her travels in Kansas were not at all what she had expected. How had she come to be in this place?

Olympia Brown was the minister of a Universalist church in Weymouth Landing, Massachusetts. She had struggled long and hard to become an ordained minister, and she loved her job. But in 1867, two leaders in the fight for women's rights, Lucy Stone and her husband Henry Blackwell, had persuaded her to go to Kansas to campaign for an amendment to the Kansas constitution —an amendment that would give women the right to vote. Another amendment on the ballot would give black men the right to vote. If both amendments passed, Kansas would be the first state to grant universal suffrage, the right of all adult citizens—black, white, women, and men—to vote.

Olympia Brown already passionately supported universal suffrage. She was a powerful speaker on that subject. Her congregation had generously given her a leave of absence for the Kansas campaign. Lucy Stone and Henry Blackwell had assured the young Universalist minister that speaking engagements, lodgings, a traveling companion, a conveyance, and a driver had all been arranged.

When Brown got to Kansas, she found she *did* have speaking engagements, but no companion, no lodgings, no conveyance, and no driver. Members of the Republican Party who had promised to provide them had not held up their end of the agreement. They said they had run out of money, but it was more likely a political decision. The party had decided not to support the woman suffrage amendment after all.

Fortunately for Brown, the people of Kansas were generous and helpful. For four months, she followed a schedule that most people would have considered impossible. Against all odds, she attracted large, receptive audiences in towns throughout the state. Still, when it came time to vote, the men of Kansas defeated both amendments. Fewer than one third of them supported woman suffrage. Olympia Brown felt the defeat keenly, but Susan B. Anthony, the leading woman suffrage leader, wrote her an uplifting letter. "Never was defeat so glorious a victory," she wrote. "We shall win. The day breaks."

Brown's work in Kansas won her many friends among those who were committed to the struggle for women's rights. From then on, she divided her energies between her ministry and her work as a suffragist. In 1868, the Fifteenth Amendment to the United States Constitution passed, and in 1870, it was ratified. This amendment gave the vote to black men, but women were still excluded, a terrible disappointment to Olympia Brown.

Women's rights advocates all over the country renewed their efforts to convince voters, all of whom were men, that every citizen should have the right to vote. Many people believed that women would surely win the vote soon. It was the only fair thing to do.

Olympia Brown continued her work as a minister, moving to the city of Bridgeport, Connecticut. She married John Henry Willis in 1873, but she did not change her name. She had a son the following year, but she did not give up her work. In 1876, she spoke to a Congressional committee in Washington, D.C., making an eloquent plea for the right of women as citizens to enjoy the same political rights as any other citizen. That same year, on the hundredth anniversary of the Declaration of Independence, Susan B. Anthony read a Declaration for the Rights of Women to a cheering crowd in front of the Liberty Bell in Philadelphia. But still women had no right to vote.

By 1878, Olympia Brown had a daughter as well as a son. She became minister of a church in Racine, Wisconsin. In 1884, she became president of the Wisconsin Woman Suffrage Association, and in 1887, she resigned her ministry to work full-time for women's rights. By then twenty years had passed since she had campaigned in Kansas, and still she had no right to vote.

In Brown's time, individual states could grant women the ballot even if Congress refused to do so. By 1896, some women were voting—but only in Wyoming, Utah, Colorado, and Idaho. Thirty years had passed since Olympia Brown had campaigned in Kansas, and still she had no right to vote.

In 1906, Susan B. Anthony died. Sixty years of tireless work had not won her the ballot. Forty years had passed since Olympia Brown had campaigned in Kansas, but still she had no right to vote.

In 1913, two young activists named Alice Paul and Lucy Burns invited Olympia Brown to join them in a new political party called the Congressional Union. The sole purpose of the Congressional Union was to pass an amendment to the U.S. Constitution stating that the right of citizens to vote could not be denied because of sex. Brown joined them at once. In 1916, the party changed its name to the Woman's Party, and they worked hard trying to defeat

President Woodrow Wilson's bid for re-election. He narrowly won the election, and in 1917, the United States entered World War I. President Wilson called it the war that would "make the world safe for democracy." Women were told they should not oppose the president while the country was at war.

"We cannot say that the United States is a democracy as long as women cannot vote," said Olympia Brown. "We are being asked to give up our suffrage work until the war is over. Women were asked to do this same thing during the Civil War. They were told that as soon as the war was over and the Negro enfranchised, they would be given the ballot. But that did not happen. Instead they were ridiculed for wanting to vote and we still do not have the ballot." Fifty years had passed since Olympia Brown had campaigned in Kansas, and still she had no right to vote.

When President Wilson went to France at the end of the war, the Woman's Party staged a demonstration in front of a fire. A frail old woman, tiny but full of energy, stepped up to the flames to burn a copy of President Wilson's speech. "America has fought for France and the common cause of liberty," said Olympia Brown, who was now eighty-three years old. "I have fought for liberty for seventy years, and I protest against the President's leaving the country with this old fight here unwon." The crowd burst into applause and cheers.

When President Wilson returned, he finally gave his support to woman suffrage, and Congress passed the Nineteenth Amendment. On Election Day morning, November 2, 1920, Olympia Brown made her way to the polling station. She was one of the first to vote. It had been fifty-three years since she had campaigned in Kansas, and she had won the right to vote at last.

Quotations for Discussion

In 1854, Olympia Brown and her sister traveled from their farm in Michigan to Mount Holyoke Female Seminary in Massachusetts, with high hopes of receiving an excellent education. They were disappointed to find that they were not allowed to test out of coursework they had already mastered and profoundly distressed by efforts to convert them to an orthodox form of Calvinist Christianity. Olympia told her parents about her religious crisis. Her Universalist mother responded with a long, thoughtful letter, which read in part,

> Allow me to say, my dear, that under the influence that surrounds you there, it would be impossible for you to come to any just conclusion upon a subject so mystified by creeds and theologians, particularly a person of your enthusiastic and impressible temperament.
>
> While there is no faculty of the human soul so elevating, so delightful, as pure devotion of feeling, there is nothing so benumbing, so deadening, so baneful, as a narrow, soul-contracting creed. It is absurd to judge of the Almighty and his disposal of the human race from some text of scripture or peculiar working of some phrase. . . .
>
> It would cause me the most poignant sorrow were you to become the dupe of superstitious bigotry—dismiss the subject of creeds for the present and be content with a pure heart, a conscientious discharge of duty, a resignation and trust in God. . . . I have great confidence in your excellent plain common sense. Use it. Don't regard the notion sometimes advanced that it is wrong to use reason in religious opinions—let me advise and entreat you to let the subject rest for the present. I am anxious only for your welfare and happiness.

Discussion: When have you felt at odds with the religious convictions of those around you? What did you do? To whom did you turn for guidance or support? What kind of guidance would you have offered your daughter under the circumstances faced by Olympia and her sister?

In 1874, Olympia Brown addressed the need of educated women to have reasonable employment outside the home after leaving school:

> But, says some objector, women will no longer be angels when brought in contact with the rude world. Alas! the United States of America in 1874, is not a favorable place for angels, nor are the men of the nineteenth century suitable companions for them. An angel in American society at the present time, would be sadly out of place and very uncomfortable. Even that hymn by which little girls are made to sing,
> "I want to be an angel"
> adds,
> "And with the angels stand."
> Nobody wants to be an angel and stand with unsuitable companions. Since women are placed here in this very practical and matter-of-fact world, it is well for them to make the best of the situation, adapt themselves to the occasion, and do the duty of the hour, and leave all angelic airs, until, by a life of loving service to humanity, they shall have won for themselves crowns brighter than those of angels. Since they are surrounded by fallible, suffering mortals, let them give themselves to the work of the world, that they may alleviate the evils which they see about them, and in so doing, work out their own salvation.
> And this is the great argument in favor of the enfranchisement of women; it is not so much the repealing of wicked laws, or the establishment of justice, although these are important, as it is that women should gain that self-respect and independence which is the characteristic of the free. Not till women share in the responsibilities, and enjoy the privileges of the enfranchised citizen can it be expected that they will gain the highest excellence.

Discussion: Olympia Brown makes an interesting argument for woman's enfranchisement, stating that women would be able to contribute more fully to the well-being of the whole society if they shared fully in its responsibilities and privileges. How does her argument speak to issues in today's world? How much of an emphasis do we place on the privileges and responsibilities of citizenship in our families, schools, communities, and congregations?

The National American Woman Suffrage Association stood in opposition to the 1917 picketing and protests of the National Woman's Party, but Olympia Brown was certain that without such actions, the vote would never be won. In an article she wrote about Susan B. Anthony, Brown reminded her readers that Anthony had dared to go to the polls and cast a vote in 1872 and that she had gone to jail for doing so. She had dared to distribute copies of the Declaration of the Rights of Women at the centennial celebration in Philadelphia in 1876. Brown wrote,

> It is reassuring to find that in most things she was entirely in accord with the spirit and purpose of the present workers. If some of our methods were unheard of in her day, we may be sure that she would approve them now, were she here, and the criticisms which we meet in our time are mild when compared with those which Miss Anthony endured.... She was concerned with the cause, not with what other people thought of her. She had the courage to do what she felt was right. More women need that kind of courage today.

Discussion: What people do you admire who have taken a courageous stance or engaged in courageous actions in support of justice and equality? What stories do you have of times when you have had to find courage to speak or act against injustice?

⑥

Olympia Brown's daughter, Gwendolen Willis, wrote of her mother,

> She was not popular. She was indomitable and uncompromising, traits that do not lend themselves well to politics and leadership. She cared little for society, paid no deference to wealth, represented an unfashionable church, promoted a cause regarded as certain to be unsuccessful. She was troublesome because she asked people to do things, to work, contribute money, go to meetings, think, and declare themselves openly as favoring a principle or public measure.

Discussion: How does Willis's description help to enhance our understanding of her mother? Does Olympia Brown remind you of anyone—either a public figure or someone you personally know—who is persistent in advocating for an important cause?

Connecting with Our Lives

In Our Faith Communities

It is interesting to note that seven decades of persistent hard work and thoughtful arguments in favor of women's suffrage did not convince male voters and legislators to grant women the right to vote. It was not until women took a more aggressive approach—picketing and demonstrating continuously in front of the White House, and getting arrested and thrown into prison—that women succeeded. From the first brave women who dared to defy popular opinion by speaking in public in the 1830s and 1840s, to the women of the early twentieth century who marched in Washington, D. C., there was a general outcry against their "improper" behavior. As historian Laurel Thatcher Ulrich observed in 1976, "Well-behaved women seldom make history." For decades, women's rights advocates hoped that rational persuasion would eventually succeed in winning the ballot, but to accomplish the goal, it took bodies on the picket lines and women who were willing to be imprisoned for publicly declaring their rights. Olympia Brown was a person who believed in acting on her beliefs, and she didn't fear putting herself physically on the line if she believed it would help the greater good.

Arrange for small groups, youth groups, or your social action committee to use Olympia Brown's story to help examine your congregation's social justice efforts. Ask participants about the extent to which your congregation uses actions in addition to words to support your beliefs. Invite them to think about how all of you could have more impact on an issue of concern if you became more actively involved, and what sorts of actions might help make change happen. Ask them to consider the extent to which you as members of the congregation hold back because you fear that public actions would inconvenience you, make you vulnerable to disapproval and ridicule, or embarrass family members.

At Home

It can be a challenge to fight for what we believe is right if powerful forces—such as media figures and political leaders—are against us. The forces opposing Olympia Brown and the other women's rights activists were no less powerful than the forces that exist today, yet somehow these women found the internal strength to make their case, to push on against obstacles, to make their voices heard.

What are some issues that you and your family care deeply about in areas such as social justice, politics, or the environment? Choose an issue that truly matters to you, and name a change you would like to see happen. Then list possible actions you could take to help advance your cause. You may want to brainstorm together as you develop your lists of issues and actions. Use your list as a touchstone, checking in with yourself and each other every few months to review how you are doing. Have you taken any actions that might help move the world closer to your ideal? Even if you are able to take only small steps at this time, are you moving in the direction of your ultimate goal?

Find Out More

Cassara, Ernest. *Universalism in America.* Boston: Beacon Press, 1971.

Coté, Charlotte. *Olympia Brown: The Battle for Equality.* Racine, WI: Mother Courage Press, 1988.

Noble, Laurie Carter. "Olympia Brown." *Dictionary of Unitarian and Universalist Biography,* published online by the Unitarian Universalist Historical Society at www25.uua.org/uuhs.

Concern for the Dispossessed

Minister-at-Large Joseph Tuckerman

After serving for twenty-five years as the pastor of a quiet coastal community in eastern Massachusetts, Joseph Tuckerman (1778–1840) became the first minister-at-large to Boston's poor in 1826. He was a close friend and associate of William Ellery Channing. Both had graduated from Harvard in 1798.

In the years between Tuckerman's graduation and his return to Boston, the city's population had doubled from about twenty-five thousand to more than fifty thousand. A combination of immigrants from Europe and migrants from rural New England had vastly increased the numbers of Boston's urban poor. During this time, Channing had become America's most prominent spokesperson for liberal Christianity. In sharp contrast to New England's Puritan forebears, he emphasized good works and the inherent dignity of all people in his preaching. He grew increasingly concerned about how best to improve the lives of the poor.

In 1822, a group of Unitarian ministers and laypeople began meeting at Channing's house in Boston to discuss practical ways in which their religion might work to improve the conditions of society. This Wednesday Evening Beneficent Association gave birth to the idea of a Unitarian ministry-at-large to serve the poor. Joseph Tuckerman agreed to take the job, and through his efforts established what we now call the Urban Ministry.

Joseph Tuckerman's approach to his mission was unique. He has been called the Father of Social Work because he was the first to demonstrate and articulate social work's fundamental principles and practices. However, Tuckerman's approach was religious, not secular. He opposed the idea of municipal or state-run charity programs, because he believed they would tend to foster dependence rather than self-sufficiency among the poor. He also cautioned that the impersonal nature of public funds would undermine the very foundation on which he believed successful social service rested: selfless giving, genuine kindness, and unconditional love.

When Joseph Tuckerman became the first Unitarian minister-at-large for the poor people of Boston, no one knew exactly what a minister-at-large should do. He had to invent the job as he went along. The year was 1826, and the city was growing rapidly. Poverty, crime, and drunkenness were on the rise. Many families did not belong to any church, and many children lacked schooling.

Every day, Tuckerman went out into the city, walking the streets and wharves, visiting the dwellings of the poor, getting to know the people, and learning about their needs. One Friday morning, as he entered a room that he had never visited before, he could see at once that the family was in distress. The floor and the furniture were filthy, and so was the dress of the woman who let him in. Lying on the bed was a man in a drunken stupor who did not wake up. Tuckerman soon learned from the wife that her husband was a skilled laborer who had a job. He could provide very well for his family, if only he would give up strong drink. Tuckerman told her that he would come again on Sunday and hoped to speak with her husband then.

When he arrived at nine o'clock the following Sunday, Tuckerman knocked at the door and entered the room. The man, who had been unconscious during the previous visit, seemed very surprised to see him. Tuckerman immediately offered him his hand, saying, "I was here on Friday morning, and saw you upon the bed; and have taken the liberty to call upon you." He did not say, "I saw you *drunk* upon the bed."

Joseph Tuckerman treated the man with respect, and when they sat down to have a conversation, he listened with genuine interest. The man seemed very touched and grateful. After half an hour, they agreed to another visit the following Sunday. The man promised that he would not taste any intoxicating drink till then. And the following week, when they met again, he renewed his pledge.

Tuckerman continued his visits every week, and the man stayed sober. After about eight weeks, the man was wearing a new suit of clothes that he had bought with his own earnings. Soon there was a new cooking stove and a clean and comfortable dress for the man's wife. She said to Tuckerman, "I have been married twenty years; and in all those years I have not been so happy as I have been during the last three months."

This story illustrates the essentials of Joseph Tuckerman's Boston ministry. He did not wait for people to come to him but sought them out. He offered friendship and assistance first, not sermons. "Had I treated this man otherwise than with respect, and sympathy, how would he have received me, and how would he have treated my endeavors to reclaim him from intemperance?" he said.

Of course, not all people were as quickly reformed as the man in the story. Tuckerman patiently made visits for years to another man with an alcohol problem. Unlike most people of his day, Tuckerman understood alcoholism as a disease, but he knew that with determination, it could be overcome. At last, the man abstained from drink for one week, then a month, then two months, then ten months. Tuckerman finally had the pleasure of seeing the man become a sober and industrious member of society with a happy home.

The aim of Joseph Tuckerman's ministry was to help people help themselves. He gave disadvantaged people encouragement and hope. Although the urban ministry-at-large was a new concept at the time his work in Boston began, Tuckerman had developed his approach during his twenty-five years as the minister of a parish north of the city. The area he had served encompassed small farms, seacoast, and islands. There was no hospital or physician in the area, so he had taught himself medical skills and kept supplies on hand. He often visited parishioners' homes and took an interest in not only their spiritual needs but also every practical problem that he could help them solve. He didn't limit himself to members of his own church. Whenever he heard about people in distress, he hurried to their side and did what he could for their relief.

Over the years, Tuckerman had observed that his own strength lay in home visits and conversations more than in sermons from the pulpit. When he accepted the challenge to minister to people in the streets of Boston, he could truly practice what he and others preached. He believed that compassion was at the center of the teachings of Jesus, and he put it at the center of his own ministry to the poor as well. It is a law of human nature, he said, that all people are interconnected by feeling. "I need not refer you to the effects, which are produced within us, while we are reading narratives of real, or of imaginary scenes and circumstances of distress," he wrote. "These effects alone demonstrate, not only that God has made us for one another, but that, *in an important sense, he has made each one of us for the whole of our species.*"

Joseph Tuckerman became a passionate advocate for the poor, which was extremely unusual for a person of his background. He had grown up in a wealthy family, and through inheritance and marriage, had acquired enough money to support himself and his large family without the income from his ministry. However, his liberal religious faith called him to service. He believed God to be a loving father, who cared equally for all his children. He believed in the brotherhood of all of mankind and the inherent worth of every person. Beyond all this, he truly loved the sufferers and sinners that he served, whether they were juvenile delinquents, people with mental illness, children living in squalor and ignorance, or criminals. According to Elizabeth Peabody, "It did indeed seem, when you heard him talk, as if the worldly society of the better classes was stale, flat, and unprofitable in comparison with what he found in what are called the lower walks of life. But he would never let you call them 'lower,' he would say 'less world-favored.'"

The more Tuckerman came to love the poor, the more he talked about them with his colleagues. The more he learned about their needs, the more he tried to persuade people of influence to provide for them. As one biographer put it, "Tuckerman was ever busy, pouring a tale of woe into the public ear." He accompanied his tales with a host of concrete suggestions. He wanted schools and protective services for disadvantaged youth. He argued for prison reform. He advocated for protection and fair wages for working women, better housing for the poor, and humane treatment for the mentally ill. In his tireless advocacy for the poor, he did not shrink from unpleasant realities. He opened the eyes of the privileged to a world most of them preferred to ignore.

Though he promoted reforms that would help the suffering and improve the conditions of the poor, Joseph Tuckerman's foremost goal was to help poor people discover the resources that lay within themselves. To him, the first purpose of social service was to foster self-help. Anyone who enters into charitable work, he said, "should know how to sympathize with human weakness and how to call forth human strength." This important lesson lives on as Joseph Tuckerman's legacy to Unitarian Universalist social action.

Quotations for Discussion

Joseph Tuckerman was a man of action, not words, and his theology matched his nature. Elizabeth Peabody quotes Tuckerman as follows:

> Christianity is a life, not a scheme of metaphysical abstractions. Its sphere is rather the heart and will than the brain and imagination. Its fruits are not words, but moral growth, enabling men to work with their hands day after day, and grow meanwhile more sweet, noble, kind, helpful, pure, and high-minded.

Discussion: Tuckerman believed that religious faith is to be reflected in compassion toward others. Do you agree with him? How is your own Unitarian Universalist faith reflected in the way you treat others?

☙

Joseph Tuckerman had a profound faith in human nature and was deeply compassionate. In 1838, he wrote in *Principles and Results of the Ministry-at-Large,*

> I do not believe there ever was or that there is a human being in whom there was or is no element of goodness; no element of moral recoverableness; no unextinguished spark of moral sensibility, which, with God's blessing may not be blown into a flame.

and

> I have not a capacity of mind or heart, of knowledge or virtue, which is not an essential part of their nature. Nor have they an appetite, a passion, a propensity, an instinct, the essential elements of which are not in myself, and constituents of my own nature.

Discussion: Do you agree with Tuckerman that there is an element of goodness in every person? Do you also agree that each of us carries within us the capacity to do good or ill? How do we multiply and strengthen our good impulses while acknowledging and minimizing our capacity to do that which is harmful to ourselves and others?

☙

Corresponding with a British Unitarian Society that had been inspired by his example to establish a ministry-at-large, Tuckerman wrote:

A man who engages in this service, should know human nature as well as Christianity; should know how to find his way to the rough heart without irritating it; to deal faithfully with a bad heart without dealing cruelly with it. He must know how to inspire the poor with true sentiments of their own nature and a true sense of the worth of character. He should know how to sympathize with human weakness and how to call forth human strength; how to count and characterize the pulsations of the mind; and like a skillful physician, to direct his attention to the prevailing symptoms of moral disease.

Discussion: Have you ever experienced having to "find your way to a rough heart without irritating it"? How does our congregational and personal charitable and social justice work today follow Tuckerman's example?

Joseph Tuckerman's nephew compared his lively, impulsive uncle to the calm and thoughtful William Ellery Channing:

> It is impossible to fancy a greater diversity than they presented when engaged in conversation, whether argumentative, serious, or playful, the one all impulse, and the other profoundly calm and self-possessed. Perhaps it was this very contrast in disposition that attached them so strongly. My uncle's efficiency arose from the zeal with which he engaged in any pursuit. His original force of mind was not remarkable, his natural powers of expression were limited; but few men threw themselves so entirely into an enterprise, a discussion, an intimacy, or even a casual project. From a condition of great physical exhaustion or a mood of entire listlessness I have often seen him suddenly emerge, like one rejuvenated, at the sight of a genial acquaintance, the men-

tion of a benevolent scheme, or the idea of an interesting journey. . . .

My uncle's temperament, his physical and moral need of activity, the quickness of his sympathies, his social disposition, and the marked superiority of his parochial labors over those of the pulpit—all indicated a different sphere, as far better adapted to elicit the powers of usefulness. The project of a "ministry-at-large," to be sustained by the combined aid of the various Unitarian churches, was a precedent the importance of which can hardly be overrated. It was an enterprise precisely fitted to my uncle's character, tastes, and ability; and this was made evident the moment he entered upon his functions. His whole nature was quickened. He interested the young and the wealthy in behalf of his mission; his services at the Free Chapel were fully attended; at the office of the Association a record was kept of all the poor known to be without employment in the city, with such facts of their history as were needed to their intelligent relief. My uncle became the almoner of the rich and the confidant of the poor. He visited families who had no religious teachers and no regular source of livelihood, collected and reported facts, corresponded with the legislators at home and abroad, and thus opened the way for a more thorough understanding of the condition of the indigent and the means of relieving them, the causes of pauperism, and the duty of Christian communities towards its victims.

Discussion: Tuckerman ministered in a way that was true to his own nature and his own considerable gifts and skills. What personal and spiritual gifts and skills do you bring to the work of making the world a better place?

Connecting with Our Lives

In Our Faith Communities
The Unitarian Universalist Urban Ministry in Boston, a direct descendent of Tuckerman's ministry-at-large, continues to embrace his philosophy of direct engagement to empower the poor and disadvantaged. Each Urban Ministry program is designed according to the specific needs of individuals and communities, not just to provide immediate aid but also to create the foundation for a healthy and productive future. Invite a small group or youth group in your congregation to investigate programs in your area that are modeled on this same philosophy and how your congregation might get involved in such initiatives.

At Home
Tuckerman believed that, for the person who serves the poor and disadvantaged, being compassionate is of utmost importance. Many religious and humanist traditions teach some version of the golden rule—the ethical premise that you should treat others as you would have them treat you. In Christianity, Jesus taught that we should love our neighbors as ourselves and that we should not limit our compassion to our own group but offer it also to our enemies. In Buddhist teaching, compassion, also known as loving kindness, is a core value. It is defined as the desire, deeply felt, that all beings should be free from suffering.

With your family and friends, explore the meaning of compassion. How might you cultivate and strengthen this quality in yourself? Do books and stories, as Tuckerman suggested, help you feel more compassionate toward others? What about daily news stories? When you hear about wars, politics, and tensions in the world, do you feel more or less compassionate? To what extent do empathy and compassion govern your everyday attitude toward others? And toward yourself? What would the world be like if everyone's actions were guided by compassion and loving kindness?

Find Out More

Eliot, Samuel Atkins, ed. "Joseph Tuckerman." In *Heralds of a Liberal Faith*, Cambridge, MA: Harvard Square Library, 2009. Originally published as *Heralds of a Liberal Faith, Vol. 2*. Boston: American Unitarian Association, 1910. It can be read at www.harvardsquarelibrary.org.

Mannis, Jedediah. "Joseph Tuckerman." *Dictionary of Unitarian and Universalist Biography*, published online by the Unitarian Universalist Historical Society at www25.uua.org/uuhs.

McColgan, Daniel T. *Joseph Tuckerman: Pioneer in American Social Work*. Washington, D.C.: The Catholic University Press, 1940.

Samuel Gridley Howe's Equal Opportunity for All Children

There were three grand causes in the life of Samuel Gridley Howe (1801–1876): the Greek War of Independence, the education of children with disabilities, and the abolition of slavery. Each of these causes consumed his main energies during some period of his life.

Inspired by the English poet Lord Byron, Howe left for Greece in 1824, shortly after he completed his medical degree, to join the Greeks in their fight for independence from Turkish rule. He served as a surgeon during the war and came back to America twice to secure donations of food, clothing, and money. He returned to Greece to administer the relief aid himself and made sure that the funds were used not only to provide handouts but also to provide employment for hundreds of Greek men in rebuilding the nation's infrastructure. He had a strong commitment to helping people help themselves. For his wartime service in Greece, Howe earned the title Chevalier (the French word for knight). His friends called him Chev for the rest of his life.

When Howe returned to the United States in 1831, reform was in the air, especially among his fellow Unitarians. This suited his personality very well. He was a restless man, always seeking a noble cause to support. He involved himself first in the education of blind children. Later, he became an advocate for children with developmental disabilities, for prison reform, and for the humane treatment of people with mental illness. In 1843, he married Julia Ward, whose story appears earlier in this book, and they had six children. In the 1850s, although he was still director of the Perkins School for the Blind, Howe devoted his primary energies to the antislavery cause. He was one of the Secret Six, a group *of men who supported John Brown's antislavery work in Kansas and the ill-fated 1859 raid on Harper's Ferry. During the Civil War, Howe worked for the Sanitary Commission, an organization dedicated to providing for the health and welfare of the Union army. This story focuses on Samuel Gridley Howe's pioneering work as the first director of the nation's first school for the blind.*

In 1833, a group of prominent citizens, including the governor and many legislators, gathered at Boston's Masonic Temple for an unusual exhibition. As the program began, a small group of blind children sang a hymn written especially for the occasion. The children assured the audience that, although their eyes could not see the brightness of Creation, their minds could clearly see God's love. Next, one of the boys recited a poem. He said that the only aspect of being blind that had made him feel "the bitterness of his lot" was his lack of education. Now that he had the privilege of learning, he could be "as happy as any other little boy."

The members of the audience were deeply moved. They listened with rapt attention as Samuel Gridley Howe, the director of the nation's first school for people who are blind, began his lecture. Society has an obligation to provide *all* children with an education, he said. The blind boys and girls on the stage were no less deserving than any other children, and they were equally capable of succeeding. As Howe lectured, the children demonstrated a variety of skills, such as reading from raised-letter books and correctly locating state boundaries on a relief map. The legislators were so impressed that they soon approved enough funds for twenty needy students to attend the school every year.

In truth, the school barely existed at the time. A group of Boston philanthropists had formed an organization dedicated to providing education for blind people. They had hired Howe as the director and sent him to Europe to visit schools for blind children, since there were none in the United States. After observing various methods, Howe returned to Boston fully convinced that he could do better. Blind students in Europe were "not taught to rely with confidence upon their own resources," he said. They were not taught to believe that they could be useful and active members of society. Howe intended to create a school that would assist them in using their own talents to become independent. "Obstacles are things to be overcome!" he liked to say. A blind child should never become a mere object of pity.

Howe's first task was to construct and purchase materials that allowed children to learn normal school subjects by touch. Then he recruited six blind children and set up a school in his father's house. The children's progress was remarkable, and after only six months, they were ready to exhibit their skills. Howe organized the exhibitions out of necessity. He had to raise funds to continue the work.

Howe and the children quickly won many admirers. One of them, Colonel Thomas Perkins, was so impressed that he offered his large mansion as the school's first permanent home. In recognition of his gift, the school adopted his name and became the Perkins School for the Blind.

Samuel Gridley Howe was an innovative director. He introduced physical education because he believed that blind children needed to develop confidence in using their bodies as well as their minds. He designed a more compact typeface for raised-letter books and oversaw a printing process that made the books less bulky. He also advocated a progressive teaching style. The belief that all children were born sinful and defiant was common at the time. Many schools assumed that teachers needed to break children's wills and punish their mistakes, but Howe disagreed completely. He himself had often been beaten by his teachers when he was young, and he knew it had made him feel rebellious, not more interested in learning. He wanted the teachers at his school to nurture each child's natural curiosity and desire to learn.

The school grew quickly. It moved to a larger building and was hailed as a great success. But Howe was always looking for new challenges. He wanted to influence the great philosophical and theological debates of the day by proving that children were not born sinful and depraved, but innocent and good. He wanted to watch the natural unfolding of the soul. When he read about a little girl in New Hampshire who was both blind and deaf, he jumped at the chance to educate her.

Laura Bridgman was seven years old when Samuel Howe met her. Born with a lively mind, she was speaking simple words and phrases by her second birthday. But a few weeks later, she became terribly ill. Her fever burned for weeks, and there were no medicines at the time that could relieve her suffering. At last, the fever broke. The little girl survived, but the illness had robbed her of her sight, her hearing, her sense of smell, and most of her sense of taste. Locked away in silence and darkness, she experienced the world only through touch.

Laura had learned to help with household chores, such as knitting, sewing, churning butter, and setting the table, but both the child and her parents were clearly frustrated by their lack of any means to communicate beyond a few simple gestures. Howe concluded that the child was teachable. He believed that Laura would give him the chance to find out what human nature, locked away from the influences of society, was truly like. He offered to educate her at his school in Boston, and her parents agreed to let him try.

Imagine the feelings of that little girl when she arrived at the school. No one could tell her where she was. No one could tell her why her parents were no longer near. Still, her fear and sadness soon gave way to curiosity. She became familiar with her new surroundings, and her education began.

Laura's teachers gave her objects with labels attached. Each label spelled the name of the object in raised letters. Slowly but surely, Laura learned to associate the spellings with the objects. Then she learned that she could spell out words herself using a raised-letter alphabet. The greatest breakthrough came when she learned the manual alphabet, a way of shaping her fingers to represent letters. Now she could quickly spell words into the hand of anyone near. With a young teacher as her constant companion, this bright and curious child eagerly talked with her fingers all day. As she began to understand the basic syntax and grammar of the English language, the world opened up to her.

After three years at Perkins, Laura could express complex thoughts and abstract ideas. She claimed that in addition to touch, she now had another sense, which she called "think." In his annual reports, Howe began telling Laura's story with all the drama and sentiment of popular fiction. His reports were reprinted in newspapers and magazines. They were translated into other languages. Laura Bridgman became a sensation—the most famous little girl in the world. People flocked to Saturday exhibitions at the Perkins School, and Laura became a major tourist attraction. When British author Charles Dickens visited Perkins in 1842, he wrote a glowing account that made her even more famous.

The amazing Laura Bridgman made Samuel Gridley Howe famous too. Yet, after the initial blossoming of her ability to communicate, after the miraculous emergence of her own unique personality, he felt disappointed. Laura's education had not resolved the important questions of the day about human nature after all. Her teachers had kept a detailed record of her actions and thoughts, but despite careful observation of Laura's development, Howe was unable to prove whether specific human traits, such as modesty, morality, and love of God, are inborn or acquired through learning. And he had to admit that Laura did not always choose to do what he believed to be right.

Today, we can see more clearly what Laura's education did accomplish. Laura Bridgman was the first deaf-blind child in recorded history to acquire language. A deaf-blind girl who could read and write, work and play, have conversations, and even make jokes, was a stunning revelation to the people of her time. Samuel Gridley Howe's persistent faith in education forever changed people's assumptions about what children with disabilities might achieve. His students offered convincing proof of the inherent worth of every person.

Quotations for Discussion

The early years of Howe's school for the blind coincided with the existence of Boston's Temple School, and many of his ideas closely mirrored those of Elizabeth Peabody and Bronson Alcott. But Howe never associated himself with Transcendentalism. He based his ideas on the "science" of phrenology, an early nineteenth-century system for understanding the relationship between human nature and anatomy by locating each "faculty of the mind" in a particular section of the brain. He was also a liberal Unitarian who detested Calvinism, calling it "the greatest obstacle to all kinds of human progress." He told a gathering of phrenologists,

> I cannot believe in the total depravity of man. And if there is one thing that is certain to excite my disgust, it is the spirit of those who in one breath exalt, praise, and adore God, and in the next, insult him by vilifying and degrading man, made in His own image.

Howe became concerned that one of his blind students had been swept up in an evangelical religious revival. Although he always claimed that his school was nonsectarian, he wrote to the parents, warning them that the boy needed to be rescued from his anxieties about the fate of his soul. He told them that he would do all he could to counteract the harmful effects of the orthodox evangelicalism:

> I shall teach him to love all his brethren of mankind; to fulfill all his human duties faithfully; to improve all his time, and all his talents; to enjoy gratefully and cheerfully every bounty which his Creator vouchsafes to him without repining for those he has withheld; and to trust himself fearlessly to his tender mercy.

And in his seventh annual report of the school, Howe wrote,

> We have too great confidence in the faculties of the human mind to admit that the deprivation of one bodily organ can destroy or repress them. Hence we have claimed for the

blind an equal participation in the blessings of education with seeing children.

Discussion: Channing early advanced the idea that human beings are created in the image of God and can cultivate and improve themselves morally and spiritually. Although we may use different words today, it is still a foundational idea in Unitarian Universalist theology. How does this idea find expression in your own Unitarian Universalist faith?

Howe greatly idealized Laura Bridgman's character in his annual reports to emphasize that, far from being disfigured by original sin, Laura's nature had revealed itself to be pure and good. In 1842, Howe's good friend Horace Mann, the Massachusetts State Secretary of Education, echoed his conclusions, writing in the *Common School Journal* that Laura

> exhibits sentiments of conscientiousness, of the love of truth, of gratitude, of affection, which education never gave to her. She bestows upon mankind evidences of purity, and love, and faith, which she never received from them. It is not repayment, for they were not borrowed. They were not copied from the creature, but given by the Creator. . . . Were other children shrouded from the knowledge and example of artifice, of prevarication, of subterfuge, of dissimulation, of hypocrisy, of fraud, in all its thousand forms, as she has been, what reason have we to suppose that, as a general rule, they would not be as just, ingenuous, and truthful as she is? What a lesson to parents and educators!

Discussion: A number of disability activists in our own day object strenuously to the idea that those with disabilities are to be held up as examples—of courage, virtue, patience, purity, or other exemplary qualities. Have you or someone you love ever been held up as an example of someone who is "purer" or better because of a physical challenge? If not, can you imagine such an experience? With that in mind, how do you respond to the Mann quote?

※

Helen Keller, who became the Perkins School's "second Laura Bridgman," was a phenomenally successful deaf-blind student who arrived at Perkins fifty years later. Unable to attend a ceremony celebrating the centennial of Laura Bridgman's breakthrough into language, she sent a letter, in which she wrote,

> With ever new gratitude I bless Dr. Samuel Gridley Howe who believed and therefore was able to raise that child soul from a death-in-life existence to knowledge and joy. The remembrance fills me afresh of the first deaf-blind person in the world to be taught whom I met in the first days of my own glad awakening. . . .
>
> Sadly I wonder why since that inspiring event so few doubly handicapped children have been sought out and led back to the sunshine of human intercourse. . . . It is well for us to rejoice together in Laura Bridgman's triumph over a cruel fate. But in a true sense her anniversary cannot be celebrated until the hundreds of beseeching, broken lives of which hers was one are healed with renewing love and the power of the mind. Each one rescued is a witness to truth, justice and fair dealing. Each one neglected is a denial of the right of every human being to education and opportunity.

Discussion: How do Keller's words call us to action today?

※

Perkins was a residential institution where blind children lived and learned with other blind children. In 1848, Howe founded a similar institution for children with developmental disabilities. He traveled widely throughout the United States, helping to establish institutions elsewhere. But after years of experience, his ideas changed. He came to believe that segregating children with disabilities from the rest of the population was a mistake. In his keynote address at the opening of the New York State Institution for the Blind at Batavia, New York, he warned about the dangers of the very institution they were dedicating, saying,

> We should be cautious about establishing such artificial communities . . . for any children and youth; but more especially should we avoid them for those who have natural infirmity. . . . Such persons spring up sporadically in the community, and they should be kept diffused among sound and normal persons. . . . Surround insane and excitable persons with sane people and ordinary influences; vicious children with virtuous people and virtuous influences; blind children with those who see; mute children with those who speak; and the like.

Discussion: Howe's ideas are in accord with those who today advocate for mainstreaming people with disabilities in social and educational settings. In what ways is the debate about mainstreaming an ethical and theological issue?

Connecting with Our Lives

In Our Faith Communities
Invite members of your faith community to think about whether people with disabilities find a welcoming place in your congregation. Discuss what you do to welcome and accommodate the needs of people who are deaf, blind, or have limited mobility and if there are barriers to their full participation. Brainstorm some changes you could make for fuller access and inclusion. Convene a small group to explore accessibility resources on the Unitarian Universalist Association website (www.uua.org) and work with the group

to educate your congregation about ways to become more welcoming and accessible to those with disabilities.

At Home
Nowadays, it is hard to imagine the excitement people felt when they first discovered that children without sight could learn to read and write. Yet even today, we may feel discomfort or make assumptions when we encounter someone with disabilities. As a family, educate yourselves about disability etiquette. You can begin with information on the Unitarian Universalist Association website (www.uua.org) or contact a local organization that advocates for those with disabilities.

Find Out More

Alexander, Sally Hobart, and Robert Alexander. *She Touched the World: Laura Bridgman, Deaf-Blind Pioneer.* New York: Clarion, 2008.

Freeberg, Ernest. *The Education of Laura Bridgman: First Deaf and Blind Person to Learn Language.* Cambridge, MA: Harvard University Press, 2001.

Gitter, Elizabeth. *The Imprisoned Guest: Samuel Howe and Laura Bridgman, the Original Deaf-Blind Girl.* New York: Farrar, Straus, and Giroux, 2001.

"Perkins History." Perkins School for the Blind website at www.perkins.org.

Richardson, Laura E. *Two Noble Lives: Samuel Gridley Howe, Julia Ward Howe.* Boston: Dana Estes, 1911. It can be read online at Google Books.

Sanborn, F. B. *Dr. S. G. Howe: The Philanthropist.* New York: Funk & Wagnalls, 1891. It can be read online at Google Books.

Dorothea Dix Fights for People with Mental Illness

In the second half of her life, Dorothea Dix (1802–1887) became one of the world's most famous humanitarians—a compassionate voice for people with mental disorders. Because of her international fame, many people urged her to write her autobiography, but she never did. Various biographers have invented stories about her parents and her early life in Maine and Vermont, but the details of her childhood remain shrouded in mystery. It does seem clear that she became an unhappy adolescent who was intent on reinventing herself. She ran away to her grandmother's house in Boston at the age of twelve, and by fourteen was living with relatives in Worcester, Massachusetts, where she established her independence by opening her own school. She was smart enough and determined enough to run it successfully for three years. Then she went to live in Boston, where she enthusiastically embraced Unitarianism. It was not unusual for her to hear two Sunday sermons as well as a Thursday lecture each week. She wrote glowing accounts of the ministers she admired in letters to her friend, Anne Heath, who was also a Unitarian. By 1826, she had made William Ellery Channing's Federal Street Church her spiritual home.

Dix lived in Boston during the flowering of Transcendentalism, but she never felt drawn to it. She valued self-control and reason above all and had little interest in exploring emotional, unconscious, or intuitive ways of knowing. She greatly admired Joseph Tuckerman's ministry to the poor and Samuel Gridley Howe's work with blind children. Howe was one of her greatest allies in establishing hospital care for the mentally ill; yet when he turned his attention to antislavery work, she did not join him. For some reason, even as her friends and associates became more and more outspoken in their opposition to slavery, Dix remained aloof. Likewise, although her achievements were often hailed as an example of what a woman can accomplish outside the domestic sphere, she never lent her support to the cause of women's rights. In fact, she avoided all association with it. In part, this decision was practical. The mantle of womanly virtue, as defined by the nineteenth-century doctrine of separate spheres, lent enormous strength to her position as a lobbyist who was "above politics."

Although she also worked for prison reform, Dix focused primarily on mental illness. She lived at a time when the field of mental health as we know it today was in its infancy, and people with serious mental disorders were the most degraded and disenfranchised group of all. Doctors who had begun to specialize in treating people with mental disorders were known as alienists, and most mental illnesses were lumped together as insanity. The term insane asylum at first had the positive connotation of a refuge—a calm, orderly place to shelter and cure those who were afflicted by mental torment. Dix became the foremost reformer of her time in promoting the asylum model of humane treatment for mental disorders.

On December 24, 1842, a surprising visitor arrived at the poorhouse in Saugus, Massachusetts. Why, on this frigid day, with temperatures plunging below zero, would a well-groomed woman with a decided air of dignity approach a public shelter for the town's homeless and destitute inhabitants?

She wanted to see if any people with mental disorders were among the unfortunate outcasts living there.

Reluctantly, the man in charge led her to an unheated room, entirely unfurnished—no chair, no table, no bed, not even a bundle of straw. A woman sat on the floor, her limbs immovably contracted so that her knees were brought up toward her chin, and her face rested on folded arms. Covered only by a few fragments of ragged clothing, her body shuddered with cold. The man explained that the woman's crippled condition was due to neglect and exposure before he became her guardian. As they left the room, he pointed to a foul-smelling cloth, no more than three feet long. "Her bed," he said, "and we throw some blankets over her at night." He was unapologetic. As far as he was concerned, there was no point in providing anything more for a crazy person.

This was only one of many scenes of deprivation, distress, and abandonment that the visitor had witnessed as she crisscrossed Massachusetts, locating every jail, almshouse, cellar, attic, or shed in which a person with mental illness might be confined. This case of abuse and neglect was not the worst she had seen.

Who was this visitor, this woman whose quiet dignity convinced the overseer of the poorhouse to let her investigate? Why was she traveling from town to town, purposely seeking out one dreadful scene of human misery after another? And why did she not turn away, as most people did, from the frightful odors, the nakedness, and the ravings of men and women whose minds had lost their capacity to reason?

She was a woman on a mission. Her name was Dorothea Dix, and she was investigating the treatment of mentally ill people. She was carefully documenting what she found, with the intention of promoting reform—and with the hope of alleviating the suffering of these "most dependent and most unfortunate of human beings."

Before beginning this work, she had been a teacher. She was also a member of William Ellery Channing's Federal Street Church in Boston. Like him, she believed in the inherent worth of every human being, and she believed in giving aid to those who are distressed.

Dorothea Dix loved feeling useful and hated idleness, but ill health forced her to abandon her teaching from time to time. During several of those periods, she traveled with Channing's family and tutored his children. She also wrote books for children.

Eventually, while running her own boarding school, she exhausted herself completely. Friends urged her to travel abroad, thinking it might do her some good, but when she got to England, she collapsed. Channing chided her in a letter, saying, "Did you never hear the comparison of certain invalids to a spinning top, which is kept up by perpetual whirling? It was very natural that you should fall, when exciting motion ceased."

Friends of Channing gave Dix a place to stay and took care of her for more than a year. She was deeply moved by the loving kindness of people who had been strangers to her. Their acceptance, patience, and concern became her model for how best to make the sick well. They treated her as one of their own.

When Dix returned to Boston, she found that money from an inheritance, along with royalties from her books, would support her without the need of a job. But—always happiest when she was busiest—she was eager to get herself "spinning" again.

In 1841, an opportunity came along to teach a Sunday school class for women prisoners. While at the prison, she asked to see the inmates who were mentally ill. The deplorable condition in which she found people who had committed no crime, but were suffering from mental disease, distressed her very much. Through the court, she secured orders for their cells to be heated. Meanwhile, she studied mental illness and visited the three hospitals in Massachusetts that treated mentally ill people. She found the Worcester State Hospital, established in 1832, so overcrowded that it was sending patients back to local jails and poorhouses.

Samuel Gridley Howe, the well-known director of the Perkins School for the Blind, was also doing research on the condition of people with mental illness. He agreed with Dix that the best hope for mentally ill people was a regimen known as the "moral treatment," which required a clean, attractive, and well-regulated hospital under the supervision of a caring and humane director. To provide such care, additional public hospitals were clearly needed. Together, they planned a campaign to raise awareness and pass legislation. Howe got himself elected to the legislature so that he could sponsor the bill. Dix meanwhile continued her tireless rounds, traveling to every corner of the state by train, by horse-drawn wagon, and on foot, to make a complete inventory of the people who needed care.

Howe asked Dix to present her findings in a petition to the legislature. In January of 1843, her shocking and dramatic account was ready. "The condition of human beings, reduced to the extremest states of degradation and misery, cannot be exhibited in softened language," she warned her readers. "I proceed, Gentlemen, briefly to call your attention to the *present* state of Insane Persons confined within this Commonwealth, in *cages, closets, cellars, stalls, pens! Chained, naked, beaten with rods,* and *lashed* into obedience!"

She included thirty pages of examples and commentary, urging the lawmakers to understand that "violence and severity" only make mental illness worse—that the way to influence a deranged mind is by "kindness and firmness." She also reminded them that mental illness could strike anyone, even themselves or members of their families. How secure is anyone's grip on sanity? The woman described at the beginning of this story "was an example," Dix said, "of what humanity becomes when the temple of reason falls in ruins, leaving the mortal part to injury and neglect."

The report caused a sensation, not just because of its content, but also because of its author. The sphere of ideal womanhood did not include politics, and the idea of a lady traveling alone to the remotest outposts in the state was unsettling. Yet Dorothea Dix was so proper, so respectable, so certain of the righteousness of her cause that she won over her critics.

The legislature voted to expand the overcrowded state hospital but not to establish new hospitals, as Dix had hoped. Nevertheless, she knew she had found her true vocation. "My painful task is but begun," she declared. She traveled throughout the United States, doing the same kinds of investigations she had done in Massachusetts, and persuading legislatures and philanthropists in state after state to fund hospitals. She also worked in Washington, D.C., trying to arrange an endowment for state mental hospitals through federal land grants. After six years of intensive lobbying, the bill known as "Miss Dix's bill" finally passed in 1854, only to be vetoed by President Pierce.

Profoundly discouraged, Dix left for Europe. For a time, she traveled and rested, but soon she was spinning like a top again, tirelessly conducting investigations throughout Europe and Turkey, and successfully urging the construction of hospitals in Scotland and Italy. She became the world's leading expert on institutions for treating mental illness.

Confronting the reality of mental illness is not pleasant. But Dorothea Dix gazed directly into the humanity of people afflicted with mental disorders. No person is so debased, she believed, as to be undeserving of human respect and kindness. We must care for those who cannot care for themselves, whether or not they can ever become useful citizens, whether or not they can ever be cured. We must do it because every person has worth. We must do it because it is right.

Quotations for Discussion

During her early career as a teacher, Dix expressed her enjoyment in feeling useful and her need for a life of action in letters to her friend Anne Heath:

> To me the avocation of teacher has something elevating and exciting. While surrounded by the young, one may always be doing good. How delightful to feel that even the humblest efforts to advance the feeble in their path of toil will be like seed sown in good ground . . . all soils are not equally fertile but I have long been of the opinion that however sterile may appear the ground it will in time become fruitful and though it may not yield luxuriantly it may be made to supply the common necessaries of life. . . .
>
> What greater bliss than to look back on days spent in usefulness, in doing good to those around us, in fitting young spirits for their native skies; the duties of a teacher are neither few nor small but they elevate the mind and give energy to the character.

Later, when ill health forced her to take time off, she spent several years reading, pursuing botanical studies, and writing books for children. Finding such quiet pursuits unfulfilling, she wrote to this same friend,

> We are not sent into this world mainly to enjoy the loveliness therein; nor to sit us down in passive ease; no, we were sent here for action; the soul that seeks to do the will of God with a pure heart fervently, does not yield to the lethargy of ease.

Discussion: Do you agree with Dix that keeping busy and doing good are the keys to happiness? Is there a tension in your own life between enjoying the loveliness of the world and taking action to help other people? How do you navigate that tension?

The report to the legislature referred to in the story was actually called a *memorial,* a term that was used in the nineteenth century for a statement of facts that supported a petition. Dix wrote numerous memorials to support legislation that would appropriate funds for the building of humane facilities to house and care for people with mental disorders. Each memorial was published as a booklet, usually between twenty and fifty pages in length. *Memorial: To the Legislature of Massachusetts,* published in 1843, was the opening salvo of nearly forty years of activism on behalf of people who were in need of mental health care. Dix began by stressing that her humanitarian concern outweighed her reluctance to step outside the usual woman's sphere:

> I respectfully ask to present this Memorial, believing that the cause, which actuates to and sanctions so unusual a movement, presents no equivocal claim to public consideration and sympathy. Surrendering to calm and deep convictions of duty my habitual views of what is womanly and

becoming, I proceed briefly to explain what has conducted me before you unsolicited and unsustained, trusting, while I do so, that the memorialist will be speedily forgotten in the memorial.

About two years since leisure afforded opportunity, and duty prompted me to visit several prisons and alms-houses in the vicinity of this metropolis. I found, near Boston, in the Jails and Asylums for the poor, a numerous class brought into unsuitable connexion with criminals and the general mass of Paupers. I refer to Idiots* and Insane persons, dwelling in circumstances not only adverse to their own physical and moral improvement, but productive of extreme disadvantages to all other persons brought into association with them. I applied myself diligently to trace the causes of these evils, and sought to supply remedies. As one obstacle was surmounted, fresh difficulties appeared. Every new investigation has given depth to the conviction that it is only by decided, prompt, and vigorous legislation the evils to which I refer, and which I shall proceed more fully to illustrate, can be remedied. I shall be obliged to speak with great plainness, and to reveal many things revolting to the taste, and from which my woman's nature shrinks with peculiar sensitiveness. But truth is the highest consideration. *I tell what I have seen*—painful and shocking as the details often are—that from them you may feel more deeply the imperative obligation which lies upon you to prevent the possibility of repetition or continuance of such outrages upon humanity. If I inflict pain upon you, and move you to horror, it is to acquaint you with sufferings which you have the power to alleviate, and make you hasten to the relief of the victims of legalized barbarity.

---

*Note: Although we now find terms such as *idiot*, *insane*, and *lunatic* unacceptable when describing a person's mental capability or condition, these terms were universally accepted at the time and did not imply insult.

For the rest of her life, she maintained a delicate balance between her need to be perceived as entirely feminine and the reality of her work, which placed her within the masculine political sphere. She did so by avoiding any kind of reward that might suggest she was in it for personal gain.

Discussion: Dix used story effectively in advocating for humane treatment for those who are mentally ill. Why and how are we moved by narrative more deeply than we are by facts and statistics? How do we still use stories to advance social justice issues? Have you ever used a story to help convince another of the need to take a particular action?

Dorothea Dix worked hard to convince lawmakers that people with mental illness deserved compassion and medical care. In her 1845 *Memorial: To the Honorable the Senate and General Assembly of the State of New Jersey*, she wrote,

> I have confidence in hospital care for the insane, and in no other care.... Insanity is a malady which requires treatment appropriate to its peculiar and varied forms; the most skilful physicians in general practice, are among the first to recommend their patients to hospital treatment, and however painful it may be to friends to yield up the sufferer to the care of strangers, natural tenderness and sensibilities never should stand in the way of ultimate benefit to the patient. And if this care is needed for the rich, for those whose homes abound in every luxury which wealth can purchase . . . , how much more is it needed for those who are brought low by poverty, and are destitute of friends? for those who find refuge under this calamitous disease only in jails and poorhouses, or perchance, in the cells of a State Penitentiary?

But suppose the jail to afford comfortable apartments, decently furnished, and to be directed by an intelligent and humane keeper—advantages not frequently brought together; what then? is not a jail built to detain *criminals*, bad persons, who willingly and willfully transgress the civil and social laws . . . ? where is the propriety, where the justice, of bringing under the same condemnation, conscious offenders, and persons not guilty of crime, but *labouring under disease*? There is as much justice in conveying to our prisons a man lingering in a consumption, or pining under consuming fever, as in taking there one who has lesion of the brain, or organic malconstruction.

Discussion: What groups of people today are suffering from neglect or disdain, or even imprisonment, because they are deemed unworthy? How does our faith call us to take notice and respond to those people?

☙

Dix gained unusual political power for a woman. The success of her political lobbying to create hospitals for people with mental and emotional disorders was due largely to the fact that her work was viewed as a purely humanitarian enterprise. In 1850, the president of the United States expressed the feelings of many admirers in a letter he wrote to thank her for a lithograph she had given him:

Washington, Sept. 15, 1850

My Dear Miss Dix,

Accept my sincere thanks for your kind note, accompanied by a Lithographic print of the Hospital for the Insane in Tennessee. The building presents a beautiful appearance, and when I looked upon its turrets and recollected that this was the 13th monument which you had caused to be erected of your philanthropy and disinterested devotion to the cause of the unfortunate, I could not help thinking that wealth and power never reared such monuments to selfish pride, as you had reared to the love of mankind. For these kind offices to suffering humanity and helpless misery, your name will endure when these asylums shall have crumbled to the dust, and the Pyramids themselves shall be scattered to the winds. Heaven grant that your noble example may, in some future age, inspire some other gentle sister to devote herself, as you have done, to the relief of the wretched and destitute. May Heaven reward you for your disinterested devotion.

With the highest regard and most sincere respect,

> I remain
> Your friend,
> Millard Fillmore

Discussion: Dix forged alliances and carefully cultivated her own image so that she was a very effective advocate for people with mental illness. In our own times, what makes for an effective advocate?

Dorothea Dix wrote a children's book called *Selected Hymns.* Two small excerpts from the book exemplify her Unitarian belief in the power of reason and the inspiration she felt in Biblical teachings to feed the poor and comfort the sick:

> Awake, awake, my mind!
> Thy reasoning powers bestow,
> With intellect refin'd,
> The God, who form'd thee, know.

> That mutual wants and mutual care
> May bind us man to man.
> Go clothe the naked, feed the blind,

Give the weary rest;
For sorrow's children comfort find,
And help for all distressed.

Discussion: To what extent are the values expressed by these poems the same as values emphasized in Unitarian Universalist religious education today?

Connecting with Our Lives

In Our Faith Communities
In addition to her work for people with mental illness, Dix was active in prison reform. Invite members of your congregation to discuss the congregation's involvement in prison ministry or its advocacy for those with mental illness, or whether it should become involved in those issues, perhaps through a legislative ministry. Invite volunteers or professionals who are active in prison ministry or legislative ministry to give a presentation to your congregation. Ask for information on ways in which you might become involved in those advocacy efforts. Alternatively, explore ways in which your congregation can support individuals and families who are dealing with mental illness, both those within your congregation and those in the wider community.

At Home
Have a conversation across generations about mental illness. What were attitudes toward mental illness when elders were growing up? What are attitudes today? Have some members of your family changed their attitude toward people with mental illness over time? Have there been circumstances in your own family that have taught you compassion for those with mental illness? As a family, support one another in advocating for compassion toward those with mental illness. Be an ally by speaking out against prejudice and misunderstanding.

Find Out More

Brown, Thomas J. *Dorothea Dix: New England Reformer.* Cambridge, MA: Harvard University Press, 1998.

Dix, Dorothea L. *On Behalf of the Insane Poor: Selected Reports.* New York: Arno Press Reprint edition, 1971.

Gollaher, David. *Voice for the Mad: The Life of Dorothea Dix.* New York: The Free Press, 1995.

Snyder, Charles M. *The Lady and the President: The Letters of Dorothea Dix & Millard Fillmore.* Lexington: University Press of Kentucky, 1975.

Viney, Wayne. "Dorothea Dix." *Dictionary of Unitarian and Universalist Biography*, published online by the Unitarian Universalist Historical Society at www25.uua.org/uuhs.

Acknowledgments

Special thanks to Tracey Hurd, who gave me the idea for this book—it would never have come into being without her steadfast enthusiasm and encouragement. Many thanks also to my editor, Gail Forsyth-Vail, who was unfailingly positive, upbeat, and accommodating, and who wrote a great many of the discussion questions and extension activities. She was an invaluable partner.

I am enormously grateful to Rev. Jenny Rankin of First Parish in Concord, Massachusetts, whose seminars, discussion groups, and sermons have done much to inform and shape my understanding of the Transcendentalists, and to the Concord Free Public Library, which has offered me a wealth of resources, informative speakers, and relevant exhibits.

Finally, I wish to give heartfelt thanks to my husband, Jon Solins, for supporting me throughout the writing of this book and for listening patiently to my endless chatter about nineteenth-century personalities and events.